BARRON'S

PAINLESS

Fractions

Alyece B. Cummings, M.A.

Third Edition

All inquiries should be addressed to:
Barron's Educational Series, Inc.
250 Wireless Boulevard
Hauppauge, New York 11788
www.barronseduc.com

ISBN: 978-1-4380-0000-8

Library of Congress Catalog Card No. 2011033149

Library of Congress Cataloging-in-Publication Data
Cummings, Alyece B.
 Painless fractions / Alyece B. Cummings.—3rd ed.
  p. cm.—(Painless series)
 Includes bibliographical references and index.
 ISBN 978-1-4380-0000-8 (alk. paper)
 1. Fractions—Study and teaching (Middle school)—Juvenile
literature. I. Title.

 QA117.C86 2012
 513.2'6—dc23   2011033149

PRINTED IN THE UNITED STATES OF AMERICA
9 8 7 6 5 4 3 2 1

This book is for anyone who needs a refresher on fractions and wants to have fun while reviewing.

Acknowledgments

A world of love and thanks go out to my husband, Steve, and my daughter, Ilene. Their tireless typing efforts, computer expertise, and loads of patience helped to make this book become a reality.

Thanks also to my editors, Amy Van Allen and Heather Miller, who worked on the first edition of this book, Marcy Rosenbaum, who worked on the first and second editions of this book, David Rodman, who worked on the third edition of this book, my illustrator Laurie Hamilton, the computer department that deciphered my diskettes, and the rest of the wonderful staff at Barron's. In addition, a special thanks goes to Grace Freedson for having faith in me.

TANTALIZING TABLE OF CONTENTS

BRIGHT BEGINNINGS

This book is a fun refresher book on fractions. Some of my students once mentioned that they would like a math book that was on an easy level to understand, wasn't boring, and explained things step-by-step, so I came up with this.

Chapter One is an introduction into the world of fractions. We'll define a few terms, change from mixed numbers to improper fractions and vice versa, reduce and simplify fractions, and build equivalent fractions.

Chapter Two compares fractions to fractions, fractions to decimals, and fractions to percents.

Chapter Three moves into multiplication with proper fractions and mixed numbers.

Chapter Four dives into division with its rules for proper fractions and mixed numbers.

Chapter Five adjusts to addition of proper and improper fractions as well as with mixed numbers. See how simple it can be with common and uncommon denominators!

Chapter Six submerges under subtraction. Besides the least common denominators, like we used in addition, we also need to learn to "borrow" or "trade."

Chapter Seven exercises with exponents. We'll practice problems with those little numbers and see how they change the value of a number.

Chapter Eight puts it all together with the order of operations. "What do I do first in the problem?" After practicing problems in Chapter Eight, all your questions will be answered.

Chapter Nine rolls over ratios, rates, and proportions. Here we'll compare ounces to ounces, figure out miles per hour, and use variables to solve for missing parts of proportions.

Chapter Ten wades into word problems. Math students are seldom overheard saying, "Gee, I really love word problems. They're my favorite part of math." Hopefully here, with some pointers and practice, they'll be just as doable as non-word problems.

Chapter Eleven continues with practice, practice, practice, and even some puzzles to play around with. Review, refresh, and enjoy!

Chapter Twelve finishes with hands-on activities that will help the whole family see that fractions are "painless"!

Web addresses change!

You should be aware that addresses on the World Wide Web are constantly changing. While every attempt has been made to provide you with the most current addresses available, the nature of the Internet makes it virtually impossible to keep abreast of the many changes that seem to occur on a daily basis.

If you should come across a web address (URL) that no longer appears to be valid, either because the site no longer exists or because the address has changed, don't panic. Simply do a key word search on the subject matter in question. For example, if you are interested in finding out more about prepositional phrases and the particular address appears to be invalid, do a search for various words related to prepositional phrases. These are the key words. A key word search for this topic might include, for example, noun phrases. If an initial key word search provides too many potential sites, you can always narrow the number of choices by doing a second key word search that will limit your original search to only those sites that contain the terms from both your first and second searches.

WARNING: Not every response to your search will match your criteria, and some sites may contain adult material. If you are ever in doubt, check with someone who can help you.

CHAPTER ONE

Intriguing Introduction

What did one fraction say to the other fraction?

"You've seen the better part of me."

WHAT IS A FRACTION?

A fraction is a part of a whole.

1 whole pizza

1 whole pizza can be divided into different fractional parts.
For example,

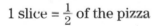
1 slice = $\frac{1}{2}$ of the pizza

1 slice = $\frac{1}{4}$ of the pizza

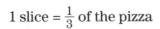
1 slice = $\frac{1}{3}$ of the pizza

1 slice = $\frac{1}{5}$ of the pizza

IMPORTANT TERMS

Here are some terms that will only tax your brain a fraction:

Fraction Parts

$\dfrac{1}{2}$ ← Numerator
$\phantom{\dfrac{1}{2}}$ ← Denominator

Is a proper fraction one that does everything right?

No, a **proper fraction** is one where the numerator is smaller than the denominator, like $\frac{3}{4}$ or $\frac{1}{2}$. Its value is less than 1 whole.

Is an improper fraction one that does not have manners?

No, an **improper fraction** is one where the numerator is larger than or equal to the denominator, like $\frac{4}{3}$ or $\frac{6}{5}$ or $\frac{8}{2}$ or $\frac{3}{3}$. Its value is greater than or equal to 1.

Is a mixed number one that is stirred a lot?

No, a **mixed number** contains a whole number part and a fraction part, like $3\frac{2}{3}$ or $4\frac{7}{8}$. The fractional part must be less than 1.

MIXED NUMBERS AND IMPROPER FRACTIONS

How do you change mixed numbers into improper fractions and vice versa?

Is it a magic trick? Not even a famous magician can change numbers into other forms without following certain rules.

(1) To convert from a mixed number to an improper fraction:

- Multiply your denominator by your whole number.
- Add the result to the numerator.
- This number becomes the numerator and the denominator remains unchanged.

CORRECT:

$3\frac{4}{5}$ $5 \times 3 = 15$

$15 + 4 = 19$

The improper fraction is $\frac{19}{5}$.

INCORRECT:

$3\frac{4}{5}$ $5 \times 3 \times 4 = \frac{60}{5}$

or

$4 \times 3 + 5 = \frac{17}{5}$

(2) To convert from an improper fraction to a mixed number:

- Divide the denominator into the numerator.
- The whole number becomes the whole number in your answer.
- The remainder becomes the numerator of the fractional part of your answer.
- The original denominator remains the same.

RIGHT:

$\frac{14}{3}$; 14 divided by 3 equals 4, with a remainder of 2.

Therefore, the mixed number is $4\frac{2}{3}$.

WRONG:

$\frac{14}{3}$; 14 divided by 3 equals 4, with a remainder of 2.

Therefore, the mixed number is $4\frac{3}{2}$.

Make sure the fraction part of the mixed
number is in lowest terms or simplest form.
Keep this in mind: You will use both of these
conversion processes later in fraction problems
with addition, subtraction, multiplication, and division.

BRAIN TICKLERS
Set # 1

Change the following funtastic mixed numbers
to improper fractions:

1. $2\frac{1}{4}$ 2. $3\frac{5}{6}$ 3. $4\frac{2}{5}$

4. $7\frac{1}{8}$ 5. $2\frac{5}{12}$ 6. $5\frac{4}{9}$

Now change these improper fractions to
mixed numbers:

7. $\frac{11}{9}$ 8. $\frac{23}{4}$ 9. $\frac{16}{8}$

10. $\frac{55}{7}$ 11. $\frac{15}{2}$ 12. $\frac{37}{3}$

(Answers are on pages 25–26.)

MULTIPLES

What is a multiple of a number?

A **multiple** of a number is the number multiplied by 1, 2, 3, 4, . . .

> Multiplying a number by zero produces an answer of zero. Zero is not being considered as a multiple here.

What are the multiples of 6?

MARVELOUS MULTIPLES:

$6 \times 1 = 6, 6 \times 2 = 12, 6 \times 3 = 18, 6 \times 4 = 24$, and so on.

6, 12, 18, and 24 are multiples of 6.

MANGLED MULTIPLES:

6, 12, 16, and 22 are not multiples of 5.

These are not multiples of 5 because 5 doesn't divide into each one evenly.

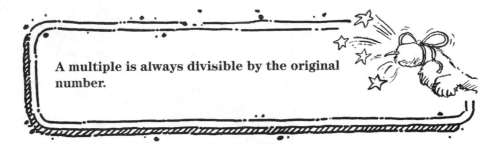

> A multiple is always divisible by the original number.

What is a common multiple of two or more numbers?

A **common multiple** of two or more numbers is a multiple that is shared by two or more numbers. Two or more numbers have more than one common multiple.

MORE MARVELOUS MULTIPLES:

6 is a common multiple of 2 and 6.
12 is a common multiple of 2, 6, and 12.
10 is a common multiple of 2, 5, and 10.

MORE MANGLED MULTIPLES:

Is 10 a common multiple of 4 and 6?

No, because 4 and 6 do not divide into 10 evenly.

Is 12 a common multiple of 5 and 10?

No, because 5 and 10 do not divide into 12 evenly.

Is 24 a common multiple of 5 and 6?

No, because 5 does not divide evenly into 24.

What is an LCM? Is it a Little Corn Muffin?

No, it's a **Least Common Multiple (LCM)**.

A **Least Common Multiple (LCM)** is the lowest multiple that is shared by two or more numbers. It is a number into which all given numbers can divide evenly.

Exciting Example

What is the LCM of 6 and 10?

List multiples of 6.
$6 \times 1 = 6, 6 \times 2 = 12, 6 \times 3 = 18, 6 \times 4 = 24, 6 \times 5 = 30, \ldots$

6, 12, 18, 24, and 30 are multiples of 6.

List multiples of 10.
$10 \times 1 = 10, 10 \times 2 = 20, 10 \times 3 = 30, \ldots$

10, 20, and 30 are multiples of 10.

The LCM is 30. It is the **least common multiple** of 6 and 10. This is the lowest number that both 6 and 10 will divide into evenly.

The LCM must be greater than or equal to one of your given numbers. The LCM will be used in fraction addition and subtraction problems to find a common denominator.

FACTORS

What is a factor of a number?

A **factor** of a number is a number that divides evenly into your given number.

What are the factors of 6?

FABULOUS FACTORS:
1, 2, 3, and 6 are the factors of 6 because they divide evenly into 6.

FRAUDULENT FACTORS:
4 and 5 are not factors of 6 because they do not divide evenly into 6.

Note: 1 and the original number are always factors of any given number.

What is a prime number?

A **prime number** is a number divisible by only 1 and itself.

Prime Numbers Under 100:
1, 2, 3, 5, 7, 11, 13, 17, 19, 23, 29, 31, 37, 41, 43, 47, 53, 59, 61, 67, 71, 73, 79, 83, 89, 97

Note: 2 is the only even prime number.

To determine factors, some divisibility tests are useful:

Factor	Divisibility Test
2	If a number is even, it is divisible by 2. *Example:* 14 is an even number so it is divisible by 2.
3	If the sum of the digits of a number is divisible by 3, the original number is divisible by 3. *Example:* In the number 513, add the digits $5 + 1 + 3 = 9$. Since 9 divided by 3 equals 3, the original number, 513, is divisible by 3.
4	If the last two digits of a number are divisible by 4, then the original number is divisible by 4. *Example:* In the number, 3456, 56 is divisible by 4, so the original number is divisible by 4.
5	If a number ends in 5 or 0, it is divisible by 5. *Example:* 25 ends in 5 so it is divisible by 5. 50 ends in 0 so it is divisible by 5.
9	If the sum of the digits of a number is divisible by 9, the original number is divisible by 9. *Example:* In the number 783, add the digits $7 + 8 + 3 = 18$. Since 18 divided by 9 equals 2, the original number, 783, is divisible by 9.
10	If a number ends in 0, it is divisible by 10. *Example:* 30 ends in 0 so it is divisible by 10.

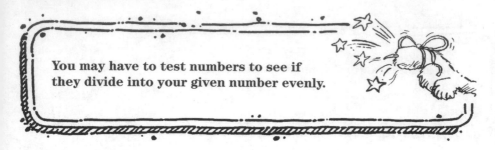

You may have to test numbers to see if they divide into your given number evenly.

What is a common factor of two or more numbers?

A **common factor** of two or more numbers is a number that divides evenly into all of the numbers.

FABULOUS FACTORS:
3 is a common factor of 3 and 6.
4 is a common factor of 4 and 12.
2 is a common factor of 4 and 12.
2 is a common factor of 4, 6, and 8.

FRAUDULENT FACTORS:
Is 4 a common factor of 6 and 8?

No, because 4 does not divide evenly into both 6 and 8.

Is 10 a common factor of 7 and 14?

No, because 10 does not divide evenly into both 7 and 14.

What is a GCF? Is it a Greasy Cheese Fry?

No, it's a **Greatest Common Factor (GCF)**.

A **Greatest Common Factor (GCF)** is the greatest factor that is shared by two or more numbers. It is a number that divides evenly into all of your given numbers.

What is the GCF of 3 and 12?

List the factors of 3.

1, 3

List the factors of 12.

1, 2, 3, 4, 6, 12

The GCF is 3. It is the **greatest common factor** of 3 and 12.

This is the greatest number that divides evenly into both 3 and 12.

The GCF must be equal to or smaller than one of your given numbers. The GCF will be used in simplifying fractions.

What is the GCF of 36 and 45?

List the factors of 36.

1, 2, 3, 4, 6, 9, 12, 18, 36

List the factors of 45.

1, 3, 5, 9, 15, 45

The GCF is 9. It is the **greatest common factor** of 36 and 45.

This is the greatest number that divides evenly into both 36 and 45.

What are relatively prime numbers?

Two or more numbers are **relatively prime** if they have no common factor other than 1. The GCF of these numbers would be equal to 1.

RESPECTABLE RELATIVELY PRIME NUMBERS:

5 and 6 are relatively prime since the factors of 5 are 1 and 5, and the factors of 6 are 1, 2, 3, and 6. The only common factor between them is 1, and the GCF would equal 1.

3, 8, and 14 are relatively prime since the factors of 3 are 1 and 3, the factors of 8 are 1, 2, 4, and 8, and the factors of 14 are 1, 2, 7, and 14. The only common factor among all three numbers is 1, and the GCF would be equal to 1.

ROTTEN RELATIVELY PRIME NUMBERS:

6 and 9 are not relatively prime because the factors of 6 are 1, 2, 3, and 6, and the factors of 9 are 1, 3, and 9. 1 and 3 are both common factors of these numbers, and the GCF would equal 3.

Note: Both even and odd numbers can be relatively prime. Whether they are relatively prime depends on how their factors compare and not on the original numbers themselves.

Caution—Major Mistake Territory!

Be careful not to confuse a *factor* with a *multiple*. A *factor* must divide evenly into your given number, while your given number must divide evenly into a *multiple*.

BRAIN TICKLERS
Set # 2

Find all the multiples less than 25 for these numbers:

1. 3   2. 8

3. Is 28 a common multiple of 2 and 7?
4. Is 33 a common multiple of 3 and 6?

Find the LCM of:

5. 4 and 8
6. 6 and 15
7. 4, 5, and 12

List the factors of the following numbers:

8. 10   9. 28

10. Are 3 and 5 common factors of both 9 and 12?
11. Are 2 and 4 common factors of both 20 and 32?

Find the GCF of these numbers:

12. 6 and 24   13. 16 and 72   14. 10, 25, and 40

For each of the following problems:

a) Are the given numbers relatively prime?
b) What is the GCF?

15. 4 and 7   16. 5, 10, and 15

(Answers are on pages 26–29.)

REDUCING FRACTIONS

How do you know if a fraction is in simplest form or lowest terms?

A fraction is in simplest form or lowest terms when no other number divides evenly into both the numerator and denominator except for 1, such as for $\frac{5}{6}$, $\frac{2}{3}$, or $\frac{1}{4}$.

Do you reduce fractions by putting them on a special diet?

Not really—reducing a fraction means changing the fraction to its simplest form or lowest terms. To reduce a fraction to the simplest form or lowest terms, find the greatest number that divides evenly into both your numerator and denominator (the GCF). Then divide both the numerator and denominator by the GCF. The new numerator and denominator represent the reduced or simplified fraction. The simplified fraction is equivalent to or has the same value as the original fraction.

For example, here's how to reduce $\frac{4}{6}$ to its lowest terms:

1. Find the GCF of 4 and 6. It is 2.

2. Divide the numerator by the GCF. Divide 4 by 2, resulting in 2.

$$4 \div 2 = 2$$

3. Divide the denominator by the GCF. Divide 6 by 2, resulting in 3.

$$6 \div 2 = 3$$

The reduced or simplified fraction is $\frac{2}{3}$.

What do you do if you can't find a GCF?

If you can't find a GCF, use any number that divides evenly into both your numerator and denominator. Repeat as many times as necessary until your fraction is in simplest form. Remember that a fraction is in simplest form when no other number except 1 divides evenly into the numerator and denominator.

For example, here's how to reduce or simplify $\frac{24}{30}$ to its lowest terms:

1. Suppose you use 2 as your dividing number (instead of the GCF of 6).

2. Divide the numerator by 2. Divide 24 by 2, resulting in 12.

$$24 \div 2 = 12$$

3. Divide the denominator by 2. Divide 30 by 2, resulting in 15.

$$30 \div 2 = 15$$

Your new fraction is $\frac{12}{15}$. Can this fraction be reduced more? Yes it can—both the numerator and denominator can be divided by 3.

4. Divide the numerator by 3. Divide 12 by 3, resulting in 4.

$$12 \div 3 = 4$$

5. Divide the denominator by 3. Divide 15 by 3, resulting in 5.

$$15 \div 3 = 5$$

Your new fraction is $\frac{4}{5}$, which is in simplest form because no number other than 1 divides evenly into both 4 and 5.

BRAIN TICKLERS
Set # 3

Reduce the following funtastic fractions and mixed numbers to simplest form.

1. $\frac{10}{12}$

2. $\frac{5}{35}$

3. $\frac{18}{30}$

4. $\frac{14}{28}$

5. $\frac{4}{30}$

6. $1\frac{6}{10}$

7. $\frac{25}{25}$

8. $2\frac{15}{35}$

9. $\frac{31}{60}$

10. $4\frac{9}{36}$

(Answers are on pages 29–31.)

BUILDING AN EQUIVALENT FRACTION

Do you build an equivalent fraction with bricks and mortar?

No, to build an equivalent fraction, use the multiplication property of 1. This property states that multiplying a number by 1 or any equivalent form of 1 does not change the value of the original number. A fraction can be changed into another equivalent fraction by multiplying by 1 (in any form). By doing this, the value of the original fraction is maintained.

An Exhilarating Example

Write $\frac{1}{3}$ as an equivalent fraction with a denominator of 12.

$$\frac{1}{3} = \frac{?}{12}$$

POPULAR PROCEDURE NUMBER 1:

1. Using the example above, divide 3 into 12, resulting in 4.

$$12 \div 3 = 4$$

2. Multiply 4 by the numerator 1, resulting in 4.

$$4 \times 1 = 4$$

3. Place the resulting 4 above the 12 as the new numerator. The equivalent fraction is $\frac{4}{12}$.

POPULAR PROCEDURE NUMBER 2:

1. Divide 3 into 12, resulting in 4.

$$12 \div 3 = 4$$

2. Use 4 to make a fraction equal to 1.

$$1 = \frac{4}{4}$$

3. Multiply $\frac{4}{4}$ by $\frac{1}{3}$ to obtain an equivalent fraction of $\frac{4}{12}$.

$$\frac{1}{3} = \frac{?}{12} \qquad\qquad \frac{1}{3} \times \frac{4}{4} = \frac{4}{12}$$

Note: Building an equivalent fraction is used for addition and subtraction problems requiring a common denominator.

Here's Another Exhilarating Example

This time, the original fraction has a numerator other than 1.

$$\frac{2}{5} = \frac{?}{25}$$

POPULAR PROCEDURE NUMBER 1:

1. Using the example above, divide 5 into 25, resulting in 5.

$$25 \div 5 = 5$$

2. Multiply 5 by the numerator 2, resulting in 10.

$$5 \times 2 = 10$$

3. Place the resulting 10 above the 25 as the new numerator. The equivalent fraction is $\frac{10}{25}$.

POPULAR PROCEDURE NUMBER 2:

1. Divide 5 into 25, resulting in 5.

$$25 \div 5 = 5$$

2. Use 5 to make a fraction equal to 1.

$$1 = \frac{5}{5}$$

3. Multiply $\frac{5}{5}$ by $\frac{2}{5}$ to obtain an equivalent fraction of $\frac{10}{25}$.

$$\frac{5}{5} \times \frac{2}{5} = \frac{10}{25}$$

POPULAR PROCEDURE NUMBER 3:

For a problem such as $8 = \frac{?}{6}$, think of 8 as $\frac{8}{1}$ and proceed as before to fill in the ? with 48.

Here's a Slightly Different Exhilarating Example

What if you have $\frac{6}{9} = \frac{?}{15}$?

Because both of the previous methods can only be used when one denominator is divisible by the other with no remainder, you cannot use them here, as $15 \div 9$ results in a remainder. Instead, use a procedure called **cross multiplying**. Cross multiplying means to multiply the numerator of the first fraction by the denominator of the second fraction. This product will equal the denominator of the first fraction times the numerator of the second fraction.

1. Multiply 6×15 and $9 \times ?$ and set them equal to each other.

$$6 \times 15 = 9 \times ?$$

2. Multiply 6×15, resulting in 90.

$$90 = 9 \times ?$$

3. Divide 90 by 9.

$$90 \div 9 = 10$$

So, ? is equal to 10.

When you are finished building an equivalent fraction, you should be able to cross multiply your numbers and get two equivalent answers. For example,

$$\frac{1}{2} = \frac{3}{6}; \ 1 \times 6 = 2 \times 3$$

Because $6 = 6$, this serves as a check to prove your fractions are equivalent.

BRAIN TICKLERS
Set # 4

Convert the given funtastic fractions to equivalent funtastic fractions:

1. $\frac{2}{3} = \frac{?}{12}$

2. $\frac{5}{6} = \frac{?}{18}$

3. $\frac{1}{2} = \frac{?}{20}$

4. $\frac{2}{4} = \frac{?}{10}$

5. $\frac{4}{3} = \frac{20}{?}$

6. $\frac{2}{8} = \frac{5}{?}$

7. $7 = \frac{?}{3}$

8. $\frac{3}{9} = \frac{2}{?}$

9. $10 = \frac{?}{4}$

10. $\frac{3}{6} = \frac{11}{?}$

(Answers are on pages 31–33.)

BRAIN TICKLERS—THE ANSWERS

Set # 1, page 6

1. Multiply the denominator by the whole number and then add the numerator: $4 \times 2 + 1 = 9$. This 9 becomes the numerator, and the original denominator of 4 stays as the denominator. The improper fraction is $\frac{9}{4}$.

2. Multiply the denominator by the whole number and then add the numerator: $6 \times 3 + 5 = 23$. This 23 becomes the numerator, and the original denominator of 6 stays as the denominator. The improper fraction is $\frac{23}{6}$.

3. Multiply the denominator by the whole number and then add the numerator: $5 \times 4 + 2 = 22$. This 22 becomes the numerator, and the original denominator of 5 stays as the denominator. The improper fraction is $\frac{22}{5}$.

4. Multiply the denominator by the whole number and then add the numerator: $8 \times 7 + 1 = 57$. This 57 becomes the numerator, and the original denominator of 8 stays as the denominator. The improper fraction is $\frac{57}{8}$.

5. Multiply the denominator by the whole number and then add the numerator: $12 \times 2 + 5 = 29$. This 29 becomes the numerator, and the original denominator of 12 stays as the denominator. The improper fraction is $\frac{29}{12}$.

6. Multiply the denominator by the whole number and then add the numerator: $9 \times 5 + 4 = 49$. This 49 becomes the numerator, and the original denominator of 9 stays as the denominator. The improper fraction is $\frac{49}{9}$.

7. Divide 9 into 11: $9\overline{)11}$. You get a whole number of 1 with a remainder of 2. The remainder becomes the numerator of the fractional part and the divisor, 9, becomes the denominator. The mixed number is $1\frac{2}{9}$.

8. Divide 4 into 23: $4\overline{)23}$. You get a whole number of 5 with a remainder of 3. The remainder becomes the numerator of the fractional part and the divisor, 4, becomes the denominator. The mixed number is $5\frac{3}{4}$.

9. Divide 8 into 16: $8\overline{)16}$. You get a whole number of 2 with no remainder. The answer is 2. Make sure not to write $2\frac{0}{8}$!

10. Divide 7 into 55: $7\overline{)55}$. You get a whole number of 7 with a remainder of 6. The remainder becomes the numerator of the fractional part and the divisor, 7, becomes the denominator. The mixed number is $7\frac{6}{7}$.

11. Divide 2 into 15: $2\overline{)15}$. You get a whole number of 7 with a remainder of 1. The remainder becomes the numerator of the fractional part and the divisor, 2, becomes the denominator. The mixed number is $7\frac{1}{2}$.

12. Divide 3 into 37: $3\overline{)37}$. You get a whole number of 12 with a remainder of 1. The remainder becomes the numerator of the fractional part and the divisor, 3, becomes the denominator. The mixed number is $12\frac{1}{3}$.

Set # 2, pages 15–16

1. $3 \times 1 = 3, 3 \times 2 = 6, 3 \times 3 = 9, 3 \times 4 = 12, 3 \times 5 = 15,$ $3 \times 6 = 18, 3 \times 7 = 21, 3 \times 8 = 24,$ so 3, 6, 9, 12, 15, 18, 21, and 24 are multiples of 3 that are less than 25.

2. $8 \times 1 = 8, 8 \times 2 = 16, 8 \times 3 = 24$, so 8, 16, and 24 are multiples of 8 that are less than 25.

3. $2 \times 1 = 2, 2 \times 2 = 4, 2 \times 3 = 6, 2 \times 4 = 8, 2 \times 5 = 10,$
   $2 \times 6 = 12, 2 \times 7 = 14, 2 \times 8 = 16, 2 \times 9 = 18, 2 \times 10 = 20,$
   $2 \times 11 = 22, 2 \times 12 = 24, 2 \times 13 = 26, 2 \times 14 = 28, \ldots$

   $7 \times 1 = 7, 7 \times 2 = 14, 7 \times 3 = 21, 7 \times 4 = 28, \ldots$

   Yes, 28 is a common multiple of 2 and 7 because both 2 and 7 divide into 28 evenly.

4. $3 \times 1 = 3, 3 \times 2 = 6, 3 \times 3 = 9, 3 \times 4 = 12, 3 \times 5 = 15,$
   $3 \times 6 = 18, 3 \times 7 = 21, 3 \times 8 = 24, 3 \times 9 = 27, 3 \times 10 = 30,$
   $3 \times 11 = 33, \ldots$

   $6 \times 1 = 6, 6 \times 2 = 12, 6 \times 3 = 18, 6 \times 4 = 24, 6 \times 5 = 30,$
   $6 \times 6 = 36, \ldots$

   No, 33 is not a common multiple of 3 and 6 because both 3 and 6 do not divide evenly into 33.

5. Multiples of 4: 4, 8, 12, 16, . . .
   Multiples of 8: 8, 16, 24, . . .
   The least common multiple (LCM) of 4 and 8 is 8. This is the lowest number that both 4 and 8 will divide into evenly.

6. Multiples of 6: 6, 12, 18, 24, 30, . . .
   Multiples of 15: 15, 30, 45, 60, . . .
   The least common multiple (LCM) of 6 and 15 is 30. This is the lowest number that both 6 and 15 will divide into evenly.

7. Multiples of 4: 4, 8, 12, 16, 20, 24, 28, 32, 36, 40, 44, 48, 52, 56, 60, . . .
   Multiples of 5: 5, 10, 15, 20, 25, 30, 35, 40, 45, 50, 55, 60, . . .
   Multiples of 12: 12, 24, 36, 48, 60, . . .

The least common multiple (LCM) of 4, 5, and 12 is 60. This is the lowest number that all three numbers—4, 5, and 12—will divide into evenly.

8. The factors of 10 are 1, 2, 5, 10.

9. The factors of 28 are 1, 2, 4, 7, 14, 28.

10. The factors of 9 are 1, 3, 9.
    The factors of 12 are 1, 2, 3, 4, 6, 12.
    3 is a common factor of both 9 and 12 since it divides evenly into both 9 and 12.
    5 does not divide evenly into 9 and 12 so it isn't a common factor.

11. The factors of 20 are 1, 2, 4, 5, 10, 20.
    The factors of 32 are 1, 2, 4, 8, 16, 32.
    2 and 4 are common factors of 20 and 32 since they both divide evenly into both 20 and 32.

12. The factors of 6 are 1, 2, 3, 6.
    The factors of 24 are 1, 2, 3, 4, 6, 8, 12, 24.
    6 is the greatest common factor (GCF) of 6 and 24. This is the greatest number that divides evenly into both 6 and 24.

13. The factors of 16 are 1, 2, 4, 8, 16.
    The factors of 72 are 1, 2, 3, 4, 6, 8, 9, 12, 18, 24, 36, 72.
    8 is the greatest common factor (GCF) of 16 and 72. This is the greatest number that divides evenly into both 16 and 72.

14. The factors of 10 are 1, 2, 5, 10.
    The factors of 25 are 1, 5, 25.
    The factors of 40 are 1, 2, 4, 5, 8, 10, 20, 40.
    The greatest common factor (GCF) of these three numbers is 5. It is the greatest number that divides evenly into 10, 25, and 40.

15. a) The factors of 4 are 1, 2, and 4.

     The factors of 7 are 1 and 7.

     The only common factor between them is 1, so they would be relatively prime.

     b) Since the only common factor is 1, 1 is the GCF.

16. a) The factors of 5 are 1 and 5.

     The factors of 10 are 1, 2, 5, and 10.

     The factors of 15 are 1, 3, 5, and 15.

     The common factors among them are 1 and 5, so these numbers are not relatively prime.

     b) Since the common factors are 1 and 5, the GCF is equal to 5.

Set # 3, page 19

In all problems below, if you find the GCF, your work will be quicker and easier. KEEP IN MIND: One and the original number are always factors of your given numbers.

1. To reduce $\frac{10}{12}$, look for a common factor that divides evenly into both the numerator and denominator. The factors of 10 are 1, 2, 5, 10 and the factors of 12 are 1, 2, 3, 4, 6, 12. The greatest common factor between 10 and 12 is 2. Divide the numerator of 10 by 2, $10 \div 2 = 5$, and the denominator of 12 by 2, $12 \div 2 = 6$. Make a fraction out of your result. The answer is $\frac{5}{6}$, which is in simplest form.

2. To reduce $\frac{5}{35}$, look for a common factor that divides evenly into both the numerator and denominator. The factors of 5 are 1 and 5 and the factors of 35 are 1, 5, 7, 35. The greatest common factor between 5 and 35 is 5. Divide the numerator of 5 by 5, $5 \div 5 = 1$, and the denominator of 35 by 5, $35 \div 5 =$

7. Make a fraction out of your result. The answer is $\frac{1}{7}$, which is in simplest form.

3. To reduce $\frac{18}{30}$, look for a common factor that divides evenly into both the numerator and denominator. The factors of 18 are 1, 2, 3, 6, 9, 18 and the factors of 30 are 1, 2, 3, 5, 6, 10, 15, 30. The greatest common factor between 18 and 30 is 6. Divide the numerator of 18 by 6, $18 \div 6 = 3$, and the denominator of 30 by 6, $30 \div 6 = 5$. Make a fraction out of your result. The answer is $\frac{3}{5}$, which is in simplest form.

4. To reduce $\frac{14}{28}$, look for a common factor that divides evenly into both the numerator and denominator. The factors of 14 are 1, 2, 7, 14 and the factors of 28 are 1, 2, 4, 7, 14, 28. The greatest common factor between 14 and 28 is 14. Divide the numerator of 14 by 14, $14 \div 14 = 1$, and the denominator of 28 by 14, $28 \div 14 = 2$. Make a fraction out of your result. The answer is $\frac{1}{2}$, which is in simplest form.

5. To reduce $\frac{4}{30}$, look for a common factor that divides evenly into both the numerator and denominator. The factors of 4 are 1, 2, 4 and the factors of 30 are 1, 2, 3, 5, 6, 10, 15, 30. The greatest common factor between 4 and 30 is 2. Divide the numerator of 4 by 2, $4 \div 2 = 2$, and the denominator of 30 by 2, $30 \div 2 = 15$. Make a fraction out of your result. The answer is $\frac{2}{15}$, which is in simplest form.

6. The whole number 1 stays the same. To reduce $\frac{6}{10}$, look for a common factor that divides evenly into both the numerator and denominator. The factors of 6 are 1, 2, 3, 6 and the factors of 10 are 1, 2, 5, 10. The greatest common factor between 6 and 10 is 2. Divide the numerator of 6 by 2, $6 \div 2 = 3$, and the denominator of 10 by 2, $10 \div 2 = 5$. Make a fraction out of your result. The answer is $\frac{3}{5}$, which is in simplest form, so your answer is the mixed number $1\frac{3}{5}$.

7. To reduce $\frac{25}{25}$, since both the numerator and denominator are the same, use 25 as your GCF. Divide 25 by 25, $25 \div 25 = 1$. Also, any number divided by itself is equal to 1.

8. The whole number 2 stays the same. To reduce $\frac{15}{35}$, look for a common factor that divides evenly into both the numerator and denominator. The factors of 15 are 1, 3, 5, 15 and the factors of 35 are 1, 5, 7, 35. The greatest common factor between 15 and 35 is 5. Divide the numerator of 15 by 5, $15 \div 5 = 3$, and the denominator of 35 by 5, $35 \div 5 = 7$. Make a fraction out of your result. The answer is $\frac{3}{7}$, which is in simplest form, so your answer is the mixed number $2\frac{3}{7}$.

9. Since the GCF of 31 and 60 is 1, the fraction $\frac{31}{60}$ is already in simplest form.

10. The whole number 4 stays the same. To reduce $\frac{9}{36}$, look for a common factor that divides evenly into both the numerator and denominator. The factors of 9 are 1, 3, 9 and the factors of 36 are 1, 2, 3, 4, 6, 9, 12, 18, 36. The greatest common factor between 9 and 36 is 9. Divide the numerator of 9 by 9, $9 \div 9 = 1$, and the denominator of 36 by 9, $36 \div 9 = 4$. Make a fraction out of your result. The fraction is $\frac{1}{4}$, which is in simplest form, so your answer is the mixed number $4\frac{1}{4}$.

Set # 4, page 24

1. Divide the denominator 3 into the denominator 12 to get 4.

$$\begin{array}{r} 4 \\ 3\overline{)12} \end{array}$$

Multiply this 4 by the numerator 2 to get 8: $4 \times 2 = 8$. Your new numerator is 8, so the equivalent fraction is equal to $\frac{8}{12}$.

2. Divide the denominator 6 into the denominator 18 to get 3.

$$\frac{3}{6\overline{)18}}$$

Multiply this 3 by the numerator 5 to get 15: $3 \times 5 = 15$. Your new numerator is 15, so the equivalent fraction is equal to $\frac{15}{18}$.

3. Divide the denominator 2 into the denominator 20 to get 10.

$$\frac{10}{2\overline{)20}}$$

Multiply this 10 by the numerator 1 to get 10: $10 \times 1 = 10$. Your new numerator is 10, so the equivalent fraction is equal to $\frac{10}{20}$.

4. Since you cannot divide the denominator 4 into the denominator 10 evenly, you must cross multiply 2×10, which equals 20 and $4 \times ?$ in the other direction. Setting these two diagonal products equal to each other, $20 = 4 \times ?$. Now to solve for ?, divide 4 into 20 to get 5.

$$\frac{5}{4\overline{)20}}$$

Your new numerator is 5, so the equivalent fraction is equal to $\frac{5}{10}$.

5. Divide the numerator 4 into the numerator 20 to get 5.

$$\frac{5}{4\overline{)20}}$$

Multiply this 5 by the denominator 3 to get 15: $5 \times 3 = 15$. Your new denominator is 15, so the equivalent fraction is equal to $\frac{20}{15}$.

6. Since 2 doesn't divide into 5 evenly, cross multiply 5×8 to get 40. Then, divide by 2 to get 20. The equivalent fraction is equal to $\frac{5}{20}$.

7. Since 7 is a whole number, multiply this 7 by the denominator 3 to get 21: $7 \times 3 = 21$. Your new numerator is 21, so the equivalent fraction is equal to $\frac{21}{3}$.

8. Since 2 doesn't divide into 3 evenly, cross multiply 2×9 to get 18. Then, divide by 3 to get 6. The equivalent fraction is equal to $\frac{2}{6}$.

9. Since 10 is a whole number, multiply this 10 by the denominator 4 to get 40: $10 \times 4 = 40$. Your new numerator is 40, so the equivalent fraction is equal to $\frac{40}{4}$.

10. Since 3 doesn't divide into 11 evenly, cross multiply 6×11 to get 66. Then, divide by 3 to get 22. The equivalent fraction is equal to $\frac{11}{22}$.

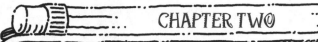

CHAPTER TWO

Countless Comparisons

Multiplying by a fraction produces
an incredible shrinking action.

COMPARING TWO FRACTIONS

How do you compare the values of fractions?

The symbol > means "is greater than";
6 > 4 means 6 is greater than 4.

The symbol < means "is less than"; 3 < 5 means 3 is less than 5.

If the denominators are the same:
The one with the greater numerator is greater.

For example, to compare $\frac{2}{6}$ and $\frac{3}{6}$, notice that 3 is larger than 2. So, $\frac{3}{6}$ is greater than $\frac{2}{6}$.

This means that $\frac{3}{6} > \frac{2}{6}$ or $\frac{2}{6} < \frac{3}{6}$.

If the denominators are different:
Change the denominators into the lowest common denominator (LCD) and see which numerator is greater.

The lowest common denominator (LCD) is
the same as the least common multiple (LCM).

For example, to compare $\frac{1}{3}$ and $\frac{3}{4}$:

1. List multiples of 3: 3, 6, 9, 12 . . . . List multiples of 4: 4, 8, 12 . . . . The LCM of 3 and 4 is 12.

2. Change $\frac{1}{3}$ into a fraction with the denominator of 12 by dividing 3 into 12 and multiplying the result by the numerator of 1, $\frac{1}{3} = \frac{?}{12}$. The equivalent fraction is $\frac{4}{12}$. Change $\frac{3}{4}$ into a fraction with the denominator of 12 by dividing 4 into 12 and multiplying the result by the numerator of 3, $\frac{3}{4} = \frac{?}{12}$. The equivalent fraction is $\frac{9}{12}$.

3. Compare $\frac{4}{12}$ and $\frac{9}{12}$. Since 9 is larger than 4, $\frac{9}{12}$ is larger than $\frac{4}{12}$.

4. Thus $\frac{3}{4}$ is larger than $\frac{1}{3}$, or $\frac{3}{4} > \frac{1}{3}$.

SHORTCUT: For the same example, you can compare by cross multiplying:

$\overset{4}{\frac{1}{3}} \times \overset{9}{\frac{3}{4}}$. **Since 9 is larger than 4, $\frac{3}{4}$ is larger than $\frac{1}{3}$.**

Caution—Major Mistake Territory!

This shortcut can only be used to compare two fractions. For three or more fractions you must find an LCM.

COMPARING THREE FRACTIONS

Put these three fractions in order from largest to smallest:
$\frac{1}{2}, \frac{2}{3}, \frac{3}{4}$.

1. Find a common multiple of 2, 3, and 4. The LCM of 2, 3, and 4 is 12, so use 12 as the least common denominator.

2.

ORIGINAL	STEP 1	STEP 2	NEW EQUIVALENT FRACTION
$\frac{1}{2} = \frac{?}{12}$	$12 \div 2 = 6$	$6 \times 1 = 6$	$\frac{6}{12}$
$\frac{2}{3} = \frac{?}{12}$	$12 \div 3 = 4$	$4 \times 2 = 8$	$\frac{8}{12}$
$\frac{3}{4} = \frac{?}{12}$	$12 \div 4 = 3$	$3 \times 3 = 9$	$\frac{9}{12}$

3. Since $\frac{1}{2} = \frac{6}{12}, \frac{2}{3} = \frac{8}{12}$, and $\frac{3}{4} = \frac{9}{12}$, the fractions in order from largest to smallest are $\frac{3}{4}, \frac{2}{3}, \frac{1}{2}$.

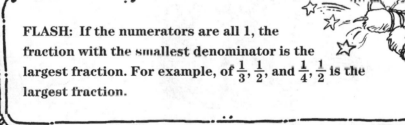

FLASH: If the numerators are all 1, the fraction with the smallest denominator is the largest fraction. For example, of $\frac{1}{3}, \frac{1}{2}$, and $\frac{1}{4}, \frac{1}{2}$ is the largest fraction.

COMPARING FRACTIONS, DECIMALS, AND PERCENTS

Now that you've compared the size of fractions, what if you have to compare a fraction to a decimal or to a percent?

It is easiest to compare fractions, decimals, and percents when they are all in the same format. So, the following methods and examples will show how to change the numbers to the same format in each case.

To change a fraction to a decimal

- Divide the denominator into the numerator.
- Add a decimal and at least one zero.
- Keep adding zeros, if necessary, to carry out the answer until it either comes out evenly, repeats, or can be rounded off to a given place.

Energizing Examples

$\dfrac{1}{2} = 2\overline{)1.0}^{\,0.5} = 0.5$

$\dfrac{5}{6} = 6\overline{)5.000}^{\,0.833} = 0.8\overline{3}$ (repeating decimal has a line over the part that repeats)

$\dfrac{2}{7} = 7\overline{)2.000}^{\,0.285} = 0.285$ (This answer does not come out evenly, so you round it off to two decimal places.) Since the digit in the third decimal place is 5 or more, round 0.285 to 0.29.

To change a decimal to a fraction

- Drop the decimal point.
- Make the remaining number the numerator of a fraction.
- The denominator of the fraction will be 10 if there is one decimal place, 100 if there are two decimal places, 1000 if there are three decimal places, etc.
- Reduce the resulting fraction to simplest form.

More Energizing Examples

$0.6 = \dfrac{6}{10} = \dfrac{3}{5}$

$0.42 = \dfrac{42}{100} = \dfrac{21}{50}$

$0.025 = \dfrac{25}{1000} = \dfrac{1}{40}$

$3.8 = 3\dfrac{8}{10} = 3\dfrac{4}{5}$

And Yet Another Energizing Example

Which is less? $\frac{1}{4}$ or 0.3?

GOOD:

$\frac{1}{4} = 4\overline{)1.00}^{0.25} = 0.25.$ Compare 0.25 to 0.3 (NOTE: 0.3 = 0.30). 0.25

< 0.3 because $0.25 < 0.30$. Also, $\frac{25}{100} < \frac{30}{100}$. Therefore, $\frac{1}{4} < 0.3$.

ALSO GOOD:

Change 0.3 to $\frac{3}{10}$ since there is one place to the right of the decimal. Now compare $\frac{1}{4}$ to $\frac{3}{10}$. To compare $\frac{1}{4}$ to $\frac{3}{10}$ using the cross multiplication shortcut, multiply $10 \cdot 1$ and $4 \cdot 3$. Write your results over the appropriate fraction: $\overset{10}{\frac{1}{4}} \times \overset{12}{\frac{3}{10}}$. Since 10 is less than 12, $\frac{1}{4}$ is less than $\frac{3}{10}$. Therefore, $\frac{1}{4} < 0.3$.

NOT GOOD:

0.3 is less than $\frac{1}{4}$ because $3 < 4$.

• •

To change a fraction to a percent

- Since percent is based on 100, change your given fraction to an equivalent fraction with 100 as the denominator.
- Add a percent symbol.

To change $\frac{4}{5}$ to a percent, first change it to an equivalent fraction with 100 as the denominator, $\frac{4}{5} = \frac{80}{100}$. Then, add a percent symbol to get 80%.

To change a percent to a fraction

- Drop the percent symbol.
- Make the remaining number the numerator of a fraction.
- Make 100 the denominator.
- Simplify your fraction.

To change 35% to a fraction, change 35% to $\frac{35}{100}$. Then, simplify by dividing the GCF of 5 into both the numerator and denominator to equal $\frac{7}{20}$.

Example

Which is larger, $\frac{1}{5}$ or 40%?

APPROPRIATE:

To change $\frac{1}{5}$ to a percent, multiply by 100: $\frac{1}{5} \times 100 = \frac{100}{5}$. Divide 5 into 100 to get 20. Instead, you can change $\frac{1}{5}$ to $\frac{20}{100}$. Either way, add the percent symbol to get 20%. Since 40% is larger than 20%, 40% is larger than $\frac{1}{5}$.

ALSO APPROPRIATE:

Change 40% to the fraction $\frac{40}{100}$. Simplify the fraction by dividing by the GCF of 20: $\frac{40 \div 20}{100 \div 20} = \frac{2}{5}$. Therefore, since $\frac{2}{5}$ is larger than $\frac{1}{5}$, 40% is larger than $\frac{1}{5}$.

INAPPROPRIATE:

$\frac{1}{5}$ is larger than 40% because 5 > 4.

If $\frac{2}{5}$ and $\frac{1}{5}$ didn't have the same denominator, you would have to rewrite both fractions with a common denominator or use the cross multiplication shortcut to determine which is larger.

43

BRAIN TICKLERS
Set # 5

In each funtastic fraction problem, which is the largest?

1. $\frac{1}{8}$ or $\frac{1}{7}$

2. $\frac{3}{5}$ or $\frac{1}{3}$

3. $\frac{5}{6}$ or $\frac{3}{4}$

4. $\frac{3}{8}$ or $\frac{5}{8}$

5. $\frac{2}{3}$, $\frac{1}{2}$, or $\frac{3}{5}$

6. $\frac{1}{4}$, $\frac{3}{16}$, or $\frac{1}{6}$

7. $\frac{1}{16}$ or $\frac{1}{10}$

8. $\frac{7}{8}$ or $\frac{7}{11}$

9. $\frac{5}{21}$ or $\frac{2}{7}$

10. $\frac{2}{9}$ or $\frac{3}{11}$

11. $\frac{3}{5}$ or 0.4

12. $\frac{9}{10}$ or 0.95

13. $\frac{1}{8}$ or 20%

14. $\frac{3}{4}$ or 78%

(Answers are on pages 45–48.)

BRAIN TICKLERS—THE ANSWERS

Set # 5, page 44

1. Since the numerators are both 1, the fraction with the smaller denominator is the larger fraction. Therefore, $\frac{1}{7}$ is larger than $\frac{1}{8}$.

2. To compare $\frac{3}{5}$ and $\frac{1}{3}$, use the cross multiplication shortcut. Multiply 3 by 3 and put the result above the 3 on the left. Then multiply 5 by 1 and put the result above the 1 on the right.

$$\overset{9}{\frac{3}{5}} \times \overset{5}{\frac{1}{3}}$$

Since 9 is larger than 5, the fraction under the 9, $\frac{3}{5}$, is larger than the fraction under the 5, $\frac{1}{3}$. Therefore, $\frac{3}{5}$ is larger than $\frac{1}{3}$.

3. To compare $\frac{5}{6}$ and $\frac{3}{4}$, use the cross multiplication shortcut. Multiply 4 by 5 and put the result above the 5 on the left. Then multiply 6 by 3 and put the result above the 3 on the right.

$$\overset{20}{\frac{5}{6}} \times \overset{18}{\frac{3}{4}}$$

Since 20 is larger than 18, the fraction on the left, $\frac{5}{6}$ is larger than the fraction on the right. Therefore, $\frac{5}{6}$ is larger than $\frac{3}{4}$.

4. Since $\frac{3}{8}$ and $\frac{5}{8}$ have the same denominator, you can compare the size of the numerators to see which is larger. Since 5 is larger than 3, the fraction $\frac{5}{8}$ is larger than $\frac{3}{8}$.

5. For three fractions, find a common denominator so that the size of the numerators can be compared. To find a common denominator, list the multiples of all three denominators. Multiples of 3 are 3, 6, 9, 12, 15, 18, 21, 24, 27, 30 . . . ; multiples of 2 are 2, 4, 6, 8, 10, 12, 14, 16, 18, 20, 22, 24, 26, 28, 30 . . . ; and multiples of 5 are 5, 10, 15, 20, 25, 30 . . . . The common denominator is the LCM, which is equal to 30. Rewrite $\frac{2}{3}$ with the common denominator of 30, $\frac{2}{3} = \frac{?}{30}$. To do this divide 3 into 30 to get 10, and multiply 10 by 2 to fill in the ? with 20. So, $\frac{2}{3} = \frac{20}{30}$. Similarly, $\frac{1}{2} = \frac{15}{30}$, and $\frac{3}{5} = \frac{18}{30}$. With 30 as the common denominator, you can see that $\frac{20}{30}$ is the largest, then $\frac{18}{30}$, then $\frac{15}{30}$ in decreasing order. Therefore, the largest fraction is $\frac{2}{3}$.

6. For three fractions, find a common denominator and rewrite each fraction with this common denominator so that the size of the numerators can be compared. To find a common denominator, list the multiples of all three denominators. Multiples of 4 are 4, 8, 12, 16, 20, 24, 28, 32, 36, 40, 44, 48 . . . ; multiples of 16 are 16, 32, 48, 64 . . . ; and multiples of 6 are 6, 12, 18, 24, 30, 36, 42, 48, 54 . . . . The LCM is 48, which can be used as the common denominator. Rewrite $\frac{1}{4}$ with the common denominator of 48, $\frac{1}{4} = \frac{?}{48}$. To do this, divide 4 into 48, to get 12, and multiply 12 by 1 to fill in the ? with 12. So, $\frac{1}{4} = \frac{12}{48}$. Similarly, $\frac{3}{16} = \frac{9}{48}$, and $\frac{1}{6} = \frac{8}{48}$. With 48 as the denominator, you can see that $\frac{12}{48}$ is the largest, then $\frac{9}{48}$, then $\frac{8}{48}$ in decreasing order. Therefore, the largest fraction is $\frac{1}{4}$.

7. Since the numerators are both 1, the fraction with the smaller denominator is the larger fraction. Therefore, $\frac{1}{10}$ is larger than $\frac{1}{16}$.

8. To compare $\frac{7}{8}$ and $\frac{7}{11}$, use the cross multiplication shortcut. Multiply 11 by 7 and put the result above the 7 on the left. Then multiply 8 by 7 and put your answer above the 7 on the right.

$$\overset{77}{}\frac{7}{8} \times \frac{7}{11}\overset{56}{}$$

Since 77 is larger than 56, the fraction on the left, $\frac{7}{8}$, is larger than the fraction on the right. Therefore, $\frac{7}{8}$ is larger than $\frac{7}{11}$.

9. To compare $\frac{5}{21}$ and $\frac{2}{7}$, use the cross multiplication shortcut. Multiply 7 by 5 and put the result above the 5 on the left. Then multiply 21 by 2 and put the result above the 2 on the right.

$$\overset{35}{}\frac{5}{21} \times \frac{2}{7}\overset{42}{}$$

Since 42 is larger than 35, the fraction on the right, $\frac{2}{7}$, is larger than the fraction on the left, $\frac{5}{21}$. Therefore, $\frac{2}{7}$ is larger than $\frac{5}{21}$.

10. To compare $\frac{2}{9}$ and $\frac{3}{11}$, use the cross multiplication shortcut. Multiply 11 by 2 and put the result above the 2 on the left. Then multiply 9 by 3 and put the result above the 3 on the right.

$$\overset{22}{}\frac{2}{9} \times \frac{3}{11}\overset{27}{}$$

Since 27 is larger than 22, the fraction on the right, $\frac{3}{11}$, is larger than the fraction on the left. Therefore, $\frac{3}{11}$ is larger than $\frac{2}{9}$.

11. Change $\frac{3}{5}$ into a decimal by dividing 5 into 3: $5\overline{)3.0}\;^{0.6}$.

So, 0.6 is equivalent to $\frac{3}{5}$. Therefore, since $0.6 > 0.4$, $\frac{3}{5}$ is larger than 0.4.

12. Change $\frac{9}{10}$ into a decimal by dividing 10 into 9: $10\overline{)9.0}$ $\frac{0.9}{}$.

    So, 0.9 is equivalent to $\frac{9}{10}$. Since $0.95 > 0.9$, 0.95 is

    larger than $\frac{9}{10}$.

13. Multiply to change $\frac{1}{8}$ to a percent: $\frac{1}{8} \cdot 100$. Multiply 100 by the numerator of 1 and divide by the denominator of 8 to get $\frac{100 \cdot 1}{8}$ and simplify to $\frac{25}{2}$. Changing $\frac{25}{2}$ to a mixed number produces $12\frac{1}{2}$. Instead, you can change $\frac{1}{8}$ into $\frac{12\frac{1}{2}}{100}$. Either way, add the percent symbol to get an answer of $12\frac{1}{2}\%$. Therefore, since $20\% > 12\frac{1}{2}\%$, 20% is larger than $\frac{1}{8}$.

14. Multiply to change $\frac{3}{4}$ to a percent: $\frac{3}{4} \cdot 100$. Multiply 100 by the numerator of 3 and divide by the denominator of 4 to get $\frac{300}{4}$, which equals 75. Instead, you can change $\frac{3}{4}$ into $\frac{75}{100}$. Either way, add the percent symbol to get an answer of 75%. Therefore, since $78\% > 75\%$, 78% is larger than $\frac{3}{4}$.

> Multiplication can be represented in three ways: ×, ·, or (). Unlike whole numbers, when you multiply two proper fractions, you will get a smaller resulting fraction than either of your original fractions.

TWO PROPER FRACTIONS

What happens when you multiply two proper fractions, where there are no common factors between the numerators and the denominators of each fraction?

For example, in $\frac{1}{2} \times \frac{3}{4}$, there are no common factors between the numerators and denominators of each fraction. No numbers are the same, and there is no number that divides evenly into both a number in the numerators and a number in the denominators. **So, you simply multiply the numerators and the denominators to get $\frac{1}{2} \times \frac{3}{4} = \frac{3}{8}$.**

What do you do with two proper fractions with the same number in one of the numerators and one of the denominators?

To shorten the multiplication process and simplify your result, use a method called **canceling**. To cancel your fractions, find a common factor that is the same as or divides evenly into both a number in the numerators and a number in the denominators. For example, multiply $\frac{1}{2} \cdot \frac{2}{3}$.

1. Since 2 appears in both a numerator and a denominator, the fractions can be canceled by dividing both the numerator and the denominator by 2.

2. In $\frac{1}{{}_1\cancel{2}} \cdot \frac{\cancel{2}^{1}}{3}$, each of the 2s is replaced by 1s. The problem now looks like this: $\frac{1}{1} \cdot \frac{1}{3}$.

3. Now multiply the numerators and the denominators, resulting in $\frac{1}{3}$.

How do you multiply two fractions with a common factor between the numerators and denominators?

For example, multiply $\frac{2}{3} \cdot \frac{6}{11}$.

1. Since 3 is a common factor to both 3 and 6, divide 3 into each of these numbers

$$6 \div 3 = 2$$

$$3 \div 3 = 1 \qquad \frac{2}{{}_1\cancel{3}} \cdot \frac{\cancel{6}^{2}}{11}$$

2. The problem now looks like this: $\frac{2}{1} \cdot \frac{2}{11}$.

3. Multiply the numerators and the denominators, resulting in $\frac{4}{11}$.

If you use a common factor for canceling that is not the GCF, you can cancel more than once, if necessary, until your fraction is in lowest terms $\frac{{}^{24}\cancel{\cancel{8}}}{9} \times \frac{1}{{}_{\cancel{20}\,\cancel{10}\,5}} = \frac{2}{45}$.

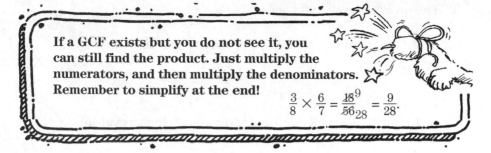

If a GCF exists but you do not see it, you can still find the product. Just multiply the numerators, and then multiply the denominators. Remember to simplify at the end!

$$\frac{3}{8} \times \frac{6}{7} = \frac{\cancel{18}^{9}}{\cancel{56}_{28}} = \frac{9}{28}.$$

WHOLE NUMBERS WITH PROPER FRACTIONS

What if you want to multiply a whole number by a proper fraction?

Nice Example

Multiply $6 \times \frac{3}{8}$.

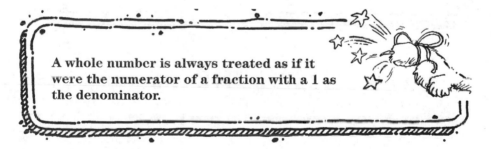

A whole number is always treated as if it were the numerator of a fraction with a 1 as the denominator.

1. Treat your whole number 6 as if it were the numerator in $\frac{6}{1}$.

2. Use canceling as in the previous problem to divide 2 into both 6 and 8.

$$8 \div 2 = 4$$
$$6 \div 2 = 3$$

$$\cancel{6}^{3} \times \frac{3}{\cancel{8}_{4}}$$

3. The problem now looks like this: $3 \times \frac{3}{4}$.

4. Multiply the numerators and the denominators, resulting in $\frac{9}{4}$.

$$\frac{3}{1} \times \frac{3}{4} = \frac{9}{4}$$

5. Change $\frac{9}{4}$ to a mixed number by dividing 9 by 4, resulting in $2\frac{1}{4}$.

$$9 \div 4 = 2\frac{1}{4}$$

. . . .

Multiplying a whole number by $\frac{1}{2}$, $\frac{1}{4}$, $\frac{1}{6}$, $\frac{1}{8}$, or any other fraction with a 1 as a numerator, is the same as dividing the whole number by the number in the denominator of the fraction. For example, in $\frac{1}{2} \times 8$, you can divide 8 by 2 to equal 4.
Note: This will work only if the fraction has a 1 in the numerator.

MIXED NUMBERS

What if you have two mixed numbers?

Nifty Example

Multiply $3\frac{3}{7} \times 5\frac{1}{4}$.

1. Change each of the mixed numbers to improper fractions.

$$3\frac{3}{7} = \frac{24}{7}$$
$$5\frac{1}{4} = \frac{21}{4}$$

The new representation is $\frac{24}{7} \times \frac{21}{4}$.

2. Cancel the 7 and the 21 by dividing both of these numbers by 7.

$$7 \div 7 = 1$$
$$21 \div 7 = 3$$

$$\frac{24}{1^7} \times \frac{\cancel{21}^3}{4}$$

The problem now looks like this: $\frac{24}{1} \times \frac{3}{4}$.

3. Now cancel the 4 and 24 by dividing both of these numbers by 4.

$$4 \div 4 = 1$$
$$24 \div 4 = 6$$

$$\frac{^6\cancel{24}}{1} \times \frac{3}{4_1}$$

The problem now looks like this: $\frac{6}{1} \times \frac{3}{1}$.

4. $\frac{6 \times 3}{1 \times 1} = \frac{18}{1} = 18$

The result is 18.

Not So Nifty Example

$$3\tfrac{3}{7} \times 5\tfrac{1}{4} = 15\tfrac{3}{28}$$

The above answer is incorrect. Instead, change each mixed number to an improper fraction: $3\tfrac{3}{7} = \tfrac{24}{7}$ and $5\tfrac{1}{4} = \tfrac{21}{4}$.

Then, multiply $\frac{^6\cancel{24}}{1^7} \times \frac{\cancel{21}^3}{4_1}$. Use canceling to get an answer of 18.

Caution—Major Mistake Territory!

Don't multiply the two whole numbers and then the two fractions.

WHOLE NUMBERS WITH MIXED NUMBERS

What about a whole number and a mixed number?

Pleasant Example

Multiply $5 \cdot 8\frac{4}{5}$.

1. Put your whole number over 1: $5 = \frac{5}{1}$.

2. Change the mixed number to an improper fraction by multiplying the denominator by the whole number, then adding the numerator, and finally, putting this answer over the original denominator: $8\frac{4}{5} = \frac{44}{5}$.

3. Now you have $\frac{5}{1} \times \frac{44}{5}$.

   Cancel the 5s: $5 \div 5 = 1$ $\frac{1\cancel{5}}{1} \cdot \frac{44}{\cancel{5}\,1}$.

4. The result is $\frac{44}{1} = 44$.

Unpleasant Example

$5 \cdot 8\frac{4}{5} = 40\frac{4}{5}$

  (See above for correct procedure.)

Caution—Major Mistake Territory!

Don't forget to change all mixed numbers to improper fractions when you multiply.

THREE OR MORE FRACTIONS

Is the procedure the same for three or more fractions?

Sweet Example

Multiply $2\frac{1}{2} \cdot \frac{1}{4} \cdot \frac{3}{5}$.

1. Change mixed numbers to improper fractions.

$$2\frac{1}{2} = \frac{5}{2}$$

   The problem now looks like this: $\frac{5}{2} \cdot \frac{1}{4} \cdot \frac{3}{5}$.

2. You may cancel *any numerator* with *any denominator*, regardless of location. In this case, cancel the 5s.

$$5 \div 5 = 1 \qquad \frac{1\cancel{5}}{2} \cdot \frac{1}{4} \cdot \frac{3}{\cancel{5}_1}$$

   The problem now looks like this: $\frac{1}{2} \cdot \frac{1}{4} \cdot \frac{3}{1}$.

3. Now multiply the numerators and the denominators.

$$\frac{1 \cdot 1 \cdot 3 = 3}{2 \cdot 4 \cdot 1 = 8}$$

4. The result is $\frac{3}{8}$.

Sour Example

$2\frac{1}{2} \cdot \frac{1}{4} \cdot \frac{3}{5} = 2\frac{3}{40}$ by just multiplying the numerators,

$1 \cdot 1 \cdot 3 = 3$, and the denominators $2 \cdot 4 \cdot 5 = 40$,

to make $2\frac{3}{40}$.

• •

Fractions can be canceled vertically as well as diagonally. A numerator and denominator in the same fraction can be canceled with each other. For example, in $\frac{3}{8} \cdot \frac{5}{20}$, you can cancel the 5 with the 20 in $\frac{5}{20}$ because $5 \div 5 = 1$ and $20 \div 5 = 4$.

$$\frac{3}{8} \cdot \frac{\cancel{5}^{1}}{\cancel{20}_{4}}$$

The problem now reads $\frac{3}{8} \cdot \frac{1}{4}$. Multiply $\frac{3 \cdot 1 = 3}{8 \cdot 4 = 32}$ to get $\frac{3}{32}$.

Caution—Major Mistake Territory!

Never cancel two numbers in the numerator or two numbers in the denominator. Fractions can never be canceled horizontally. One number must be from the numerator and one number must be from the denominator.

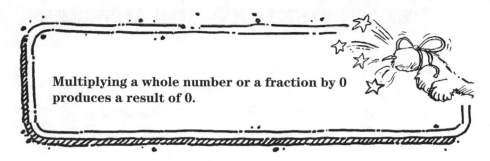

Multiplying a whole number or a fraction by 0 produces a result of 0.

BRAIN TICKLERS
Set # 6

Multiply the following funtastic fractions. Change all improper fraction answers to mixed numbers:

1. $\frac{2}{5} \times \frac{5}{7}$ 2. $\frac{2}{5} \times \frac{15}{28}$ 3. $6 \cdot \frac{4}{5}$

4. $1\frac{1}{4} \times 16$ 5. $5\frac{3}{5} \cdot 3\frac{1}{3}$ 6. $\frac{5}{9} \cdot 2\frac{2}{3}$

7. $\frac{1}{3} \cdot \frac{2}{5} \cdot \frac{5}{8}$ 8. $\frac{2}{3} \times \frac{4}{10}$ 9. $2\frac{1}{6} \times 1\frac{3}{5}$

10. $\frac{8}{9} \cdot 18$

(Answers are on pages 60–62.)

BRAIN TICKLERS—THE ANSWERS

Set # 6, page 59

1. Cancel the 5 in the numerator with the 5 in the denominator, $\frac{2}{1\cancel{5}} \cdot \frac{\cancel{5}^1}{7}$. Multiply your numerators, $2 \cdot 1 = 2$, and your denominators, $1 \cdot 7 = 7$. Your answer is $\frac{2}{7}$.

2. Since 2 divides evenly into both 2 and 28, and 5 divides evenly into both 5 and 15, you can use canceling, $\frac{1\cancel{2}}{1\cancel{5}} \cdot \frac{\cancel{15}^3}{\cancel{28}\,14}$, to simplify your answer. Multiply your numerators, $1 \cdot 3 = 3$, and your denominators, $1 \cdot 14 = 14$. Your answer is $\frac{3}{14}$.

3. There is no common factor between the numerator and denominator. Treat the whole number 6 as if it were in the numerator because $6 = \frac{6}{1}$ and multiply it by 4, $6 \cdot 4 = 24$. The denominator is 5, so your answer is $\frac{24}{5}$. You can change this to a mixed number by dividing 5 into 24 to equal $4\frac{4}{5}$.

4. Change $1\frac{1}{4}$ to an improper fraction. $4 \cdot 1 + 1 = 5$ for the numerator, and 4 remains the denominator. So, $1\frac{1}{4} = \frac{5}{4}$. Multiply $\frac{5}{4} \cdot 16$. Use canceling for 4 and 16 because 4 divides evenly into both, $\frac{5}{1\cancel{4}} \cdot \cancel{16}^4$. Multiply the remaining numbers to get an answer of 20.

5. Change $5\frac{3}{5}$ to an improper fraction: $5 \cdot 5 + 3 = 28$ for the numerator and 5 remains the denominator. So, $5\frac{3}{5} = \frac{28}{5}$. Also change $3\frac{1}{3}$ to an improper fraction: $3 \cdot 3 + 1 = 10$ for the numerator, and 3 remains the denominator. So, $3\frac{1}{3} = \frac{10}{3}$. Multiply $\frac{28}{5} \cdot \frac{10}{3}$. Use canceling to divide 5 into both 5 and 10, $\frac{28}{\cancel{5}^1} \cdot \frac{\cancel{10}^2}{3}$. Multiply the remaining numbers to get an answer of $\frac{56}{3}$. Change this to a mixed number by dividing 3 into 56 to get $18\frac{2}{3}$.

6. Change $2\frac{2}{3}$ to an improper fraction: $3 \cdot 2 + 2 = 8$ for the numerator, and 3 remains the denominator. So, $2\frac{2}{3} = \frac{8}{3}$. Multiply $\frac{5}{9} \cdot \frac{8}{3}$. There are no common factors between the numerators and the denominators, so multiply $5 \cdot 8$ in the numerator and $9 \cdot 3$ in the denominator to get an answer of $\frac{40}{27}$. Change to a mixed number by dividing 27 into 40 to get $1\frac{13}{27}$.

7. Here, the 5 in the second denominator and the 5 in the third numerator can be canceled, $\frac{1}{3} \cdot \frac{2}{\cancel{5}^1} \cdot \frac{\cancel{5}^1}{8}$. Next, use canceling to divide 2 into itself in the second numerator and into 8 in the third denominator, $\frac{1}{3} \cdot \frac{\cancel{2}^1}{1} \cdot \frac{1}{\cancel{8}_4}$. Multiply the remaining numbers in the numerator to get 1 and in the denominator to get 12. Your resulting fraction is $\frac{1}{12}$.

8. In $\frac{2}{3} \cdot \frac{4}{10}$, you can use canceling in one of two ways:
(1) Divide 2 into itself and into 10 on a diagonal, $\frac{1\cancel{2}}{3} \cdot \frac{4}{\cancel{10}5}$.
Now multiply your numerators, $1 \cdot 4 = 4$, and your denominators, $3 \cdot 5 = 15$. Your answer is $\frac{4}{15}$. (2) In the second method, you can cancel in an up/down fashion in the second fraction. Divide 2 into 4 and 2 into 10, $\frac{2}{3} \cdot \frac{\cancel{4}2}{\cancel{10}5}$. Now multiply your numerators, $2 \cdot 2 = 4$, and your denominators, $3 \cdot 5 = 15$. Your answer is $\frac{4}{15}$.

9. Change $2\frac{1}{6}$ to an improper fraction. $6 \cdot 2 + 1 = 13$ for the numerator, and 6 remains the denominator. So, $2\frac{1}{6} = \frac{13}{6}$. Now, change $1\frac{3}{5}$ to an improper fraction. $5 \cdot 1 + 3 = 8$ for the numerator, and 5 remains the denominator. So, $1\frac{3}{5} = \frac{8}{5}$. You now have $\frac{13}{6} \cdot \frac{8}{5}$. Use canceling to divide 2 into both 6 and 8, $\frac{13}{\cancel{6}3} \cdot \frac{\cancel{8}4}{5}$. Your product now looks like $\frac{13}{3} \cdot \frac{4}{5}$. Multiply your numerators, $13 \cdot 4 = 52$, and your denominators $3 \cdot 5 = 15$. Your fraction is $\frac{52}{15}$. Divide 15 into 52 to get $3\frac{7}{15}$.

10. Change the whole number to $\frac{18}{1}$. Use canceling to divide 9 into both 9 and 18, $\frac{8}{\cancel{9}1} \times \frac{\cancel{18}2}{1}$. The problem now looks like $\frac{8}{1} \times \frac{2}{1}$. Multiply to get $\frac{16}{1}$, or 16.

CHAPTER FOUR

Dazzling Division in a Fraction of the Time

When you divide whole numbers
Your result is quite small,
But we fractions when divided,
Yield a larger result after all.

A **reciprocal** of a fraction is a fraction where the numerator and denominator are reversed from the original.

EXAMPLE:

$\frac{2}{3}$ and $\frac{3}{2}$ are reciprocals

EXAMPLE:

$\frac{1}{4}$ and 4 are reciprocals

Caution—Major Mistake Territory!

The reciprocal of $2\frac{3}{5} \neq 2\frac{5}{3}$. The definition of reciprocals applies to proper and improper fractions, not a fraction included as part of a mixed number.

A fraction multiplied by its reciprocal equals 1. To divide two fractions, multiply the first fraction by the reciprocal of the second fraction. Then, use the rules for multiplication of fractions.

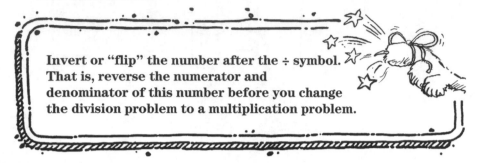

Invert or "flip" the number after the ÷ symbol. That is, reverse the numerator and denominator of this number before you change the division problem to a multiplication problem.

TWO PROPER FRACTIONS

How do I divide two proper fractions?

Superb Example

Find $\frac{1}{2} \div \frac{1}{3}$.

1. Change the second fraction $\frac{1}{3}$ to $\frac{3}{1}$, because $\frac{3}{1}$ is the reciprocal of $\frac{1}{3}$.

2. Change the division symbol ÷ to a multiplication symbol ×, ·, or ( ).

3. Use multiplication rules and simplify your answer. The problem now looks like $\frac{1}{2} \cdot \frac{3}{1} = \frac{3}{2}$, which equals $1\frac{1}{2}$.

Silly Example

$\frac{1}{2} \div \frac{1}{3} = \frac{1}{6}$

You can't multiply the two numerators and the denominators in a division problem.

TWO MIXED NUMBERS

What about two mixed numbers?

Divine Example

Find $3\frac{1}{2} \div 2\frac{3}{4}$.

1. Change **mixed numbers** to **improper fractions**.

$$3\frac{1}{2} = \frac{7}{2} \qquad\qquad 2\frac{3}{4} = \frac{11}{4}$$

2. The problem now looks like $\frac{7}{2} \div \frac{11}{4}$.

3. Change the $\frac{11}{4}$ to $\frac{4}{11}$ and the division symbol to multiplication.

4. The problem now looks like $\frac{7}{2} \times \frac{4}{11}$.

5. Cancel the 2 and 4 because $4 \div 2 = 2$ and $2 \div 2 = 1$:
$$\frac{7}{1\overset{}{2}} \times \frac{4^{2}}{11}.$$

6. The problem now looks like $\frac{7}{1} \times \frac{2}{11}$.

7. Use multiplication rules to simplify your answer. $\frac{7 \times 2 = 14}{1 \times 11 = 11}$.
Your answer is $\frac{14}{11}$, which equals $1\frac{3}{11}$.

DISASTROUS:

$$3\frac{1}{2} \div 2\frac{3}{4} = \frac{7}{2} \times \frac{11}{4} = \frac{77}{8} = 9\frac{5}{8}$$

MORE DISASTROUS:

$$3\frac{1}{2} \div 2\frac{3}{4} = 3\frac{1}{2} \times 2\frac{3}{4} = 6\frac{3}{8}$$

MOST DISASTROUS:

$$3\frac{1}{2} \div 2\frac{3}{4} = 3\frac{2}{1} \times 2\frac{4}{3} = 6\frac{8}{3}$$

THREE REMINDERS FOR DIVISION:

1. For mixed numbers, don't multiply or divide the two whole numbers and then the two fractions.
2. Change all mixed numbers to improper fractions.
3. Flip or invert the fraction after the division symbol ÷ to its reciprocal before you multiply.

WHOLE NUMBER AND PROPER FRACTION

What about a whole number and a proper fraction?

Awesome Example

Find $6 \div \frac{2}{7}$.

1. Invert the $\frac{2}{7}$ to $\frac{7}{2}$, because $\frac{7}{2}$ is the reciprocal of $\frac{2}{7}$.

2. Cancel the 2 and the 6 by dividing 2 into each number.

$$6 \div 2 = 3 \qquad \overset{3}{6} \times \frac{7}{\underset{1}{2}}$$
$$2 \div 2 = 1$$

3. The problem now looks like $3 \times \frac{7}{1}$. The answer is 21.

AWFUL:

$$6 \div \frac{2}{7} = \frac{1}{6} \times \frac{2}{7} = \frac{2}{42} = \frac{1}{21}$$

MIXED NUMBER AND WHOLE NUMBER

How do I handle a mixed number and a whole number?

Get a grip on it of course.

Fabulous Example

Find $1\frac{2}{7} \div 6$.

1. Change the $1\frac{2}{7}$ to the improper fraction $\frac{9}{7}$.

2. Think of 6 as $\frac{6}{1}$ and invert it to $\frac{1}{6}$.

3. The problem now looks like $\frac{9}{7} \times \frac{1}{6}$.

4. Use canceling (by dividing 3 into both 6 and 9).

$$6 \div 3 = 2 \qquad \frac{^3\cancel{9}}{7} \times \frac{1}{\cancel{6}_2}$$

$$9 \div 3 = 3$$

5. The problem now looks like $\frac{3}{7} \times \frac{1}{2}$.

6. Use multiplication rules to simplify your answer:

$$\frac{3 \times 1 = 3}{7 \times 2 = 14}.$$

Your answer is $\frac{3}{14}$.

FRAUDULENT:

$$1\frac{2}{7} \div 6 = \frac{9}{7} \cdot 6 = \frac{54}{7} = 7\frac{5}{7}$$

Caution—Major Mistake Territory!

0 in the numerator of a fraction makes the fraction equal to 0.
0 in the denominator of a fraction makes the fraction "undefined" because you can't divide by 0.

EXAMPLE:

$\frac{0}{6} = 0$ because $6\overline{)0}^{\,0}$ and $0 \cdot 6 = 0$ to check

EXAMPLE:

$\frac{6}{0} =$ undefined because $0\overline{)6}^{\,?}$ and there is no number that can be multiplied by 0 to give you 6.

BRAIN TICKLERS
Set # 7

Divide the following funtastic fractions:

1. $\frac{2}{5} \div \frac{8}{3}$ 2. $\frac{2}{5} \div 5$ 3. $5 \div 1\frac{2}{5}$

4. $7\frac{1}{2} \div 2\frac{2}{9}$ 5. $1\frac{1}{6} \div \frac{3}{4}$ 6. $2\frac{3}{5} \div 3\frac{3}{10}$

7. $\frac{6}{5} \div \frac{1}{3}$ 8. $\frac{7}{8} \div 2$ 9. $2\frac{1}{4} \div 1\frac{3}{8}$

10. $\frac{7}{3} \div 2\frac{4}{5}$

(Answers are on pages 72–74.)

BRAIN TICKLERS—THE ANSWERS

Set # 7, page 71

1. Invert the number after the ÷ symbol to its reciprocal of $\frac{3}{8}$. Change the problem to multiplication, $\frac{2}{5} \times \frac{3}{8}$. Use canceling to divide 2 into both 2 and 8, $\frac{\overset{1}{2}}{5} \times \frac{3}{\underset{4}{8}}$. Multiply the remaining numerators, $1 \cdot 3 = 3$, and the remaining denominators, $5 \cdot 4 = 20$. Your answer is $\frac{3}{20}$.

2. Invert the whole number 5 to its reciprocal of $\frac{1}{5}$. Change the problem to multiplication, $\frac{2}{5} \times \frac{1}{5}$. There are no common factors, so multiply the numerators, $2 \cdot 1 = 2$, and the denominators, $5 \cdot 5 = 25$. Your answer is $\frac{2}{25}$.

3. Change $1\frac{2}{5}$ to an improper fraction, $5 \cdot 1 + 2 = 7$ is the numerator, and 5 remains as the denominator. So, $1\frac{2}{5} = \frac{7}{5}$. The problem now reads $5 \div \frac{7}{5}$. Invert $\frac{7}{5}$ to its reciprocal of $\frac{5}{7}$ and change the problem to multiplication, $5 \times \frac{5}{7}$. Multiply $5 \cdot 5$ to get a numerator of 25. The denominator remains 7. The result is $\frac{25}{7}$. Change this to the mixed number of $3\frac{4}{7}$ by dividing 7 into 25. Your answer, as a mixed number, is $3\frac{4}{7}$.

4. Change $7\frac{1}{2}$ to an improper fraction: $2 \cdot 7 + 1 = 15$ is the numerator, and 2 remains as the denominator. The fraction becomes $\frac{15}{2}$. Change $2\frac{2}{9}$ to an improper fraction: $9 \cdot 2 + 2 = 20$ is the numerator, and 9 remains the denominator. The fraction becomes $\frac{20}{9}$. The problem now looks like $\frac{15}{2} \div \frac{20}{9}$. Invert $\frac{20}{9}$ to its reciprocal of $\frac{9}{20}$ and change the problem to multiplication, $\frac{15}{2} \times \frac{9}{20}$. Since 5 divides evenly into both 15 and 20, $15 \div 5 = 3$ and $20 \div 5 = 4$, use canceling to simplify: $\frac{\overset{3}{15}}{2} \times \frac{9}{\underset{4}{20}}$. Multiply the numerators, $3 \cdot 9 = 27$, and the denominators, $2 \cdot 4 = 8$. The result is $\frac{27}{8}$. Change this to a mixed number by dividing 8 into 27. Your answer is $3\frac{3}{8}$.

5. Change $1\frac{1}{6}$ to an improper fraction, $6 \cdot 1 + 1 = 7$ is the numerator, and 6 remains as the denominator. The fraction becomes $\frac{7}{6}$. The problem now reads $\frac{7}{6} \div \frac{3}{4}$. Invert the second fraction to its reciprocal of $\frac{4}{3}$ and multiply. The problem now looks like $\frac{7}{6} \times \frac{4}{3}$. Since 2 is a common factor to both 4 and 6, $4 \div 2 = 2$ and $6 \div 2 = 3$, you can use canceling to simplify, $\frac{7}{\overset{}{\underset{3}{6}}} \times \frac{\overset{2}{4}}{3}$. Multiply the numerators, $7 \cdot 2 = 14$, and the denominators, $3 \cdot 3 = 9$. The result is $\frac{14}{9}$. To change $\frac{14}{9}$ to a mixed number, divide 9 into 14. The answer is $1\frac{5}{9}$.

6. Change $2\frac{3}{5}$ to the improper fraction $\frac{13}{5}$: $5 \cdot 2 + 3 = 13$, and 5 remains as the denominator. Change $3\frac{3}{10}$ to the improper fraction $\frac{33}{10}$: $10 \cdot 3 + 3 = 33$, and 10 remains as the denominator. The problem now looks like $\frac{13}{5} \div \frac{33}{10}$. Invert $\frac{33}{10}$ to its reciprocal of $\frac{10}{33}$ and multiply, $\frac{13}{5} \times \frac{10}{33}$. Since 5 is a common factor to both 5 and 10, you can use canceling to simplify, $\frac{13}{\underset{1}{5}} \times \frac{\overset{2}{10}}{33}$. Multiply $13 \cdot 2$ in the numerator to equal 26, and $1 \cdot 33$ in the denominator to equal 33. Your answer is $\frac{26}{33}$.

7. Invert $\frac{1}{3}$ to its reciprocal of $\frac{3}{1}$, or 3. Change the problem to multiplication, $\frac{6}{5} \times \frac{3}{1}$. Multiply $6 \cdot 3$ in the numerator to equal 18, and $5 \cdot 1$ in the denominator to equal 5. You now have the improper fraction $\frac{18}{5}$. Change this improper fraction to the mixed number $3\frac{3}{5}$.

8. Invert 2 to its reciprocal of $\frac{1}{2}$ and multiply. The problem now looks like $\frac{7}{8} \times \frac{1}{2}$. Multiply to get $\frac{7 \times 1}{8 \times 2} = \frac{7}{16}$.

9. Change $2\frac{1}{4}$ to the improper fraction $\frac{9}{4}$: $4\cdot 2 + 1 = 9$, and 4 remains as the denominator. Change $1\frac{3}{8}$ to the improper fraction, $\frac{11}{8}$: $8\cdot 1 + 3 = 11$, and 8 remains the denominator. The problem now looks like $\frac{9}{4} \div \frac{11}{8}$. Invert $\frac{11}{8}$ to its reciprocal of $\frac{8}{11}$ and change the problem to multiplication. The problem now looks like $\frac{9}{4} \times \frac{8}{11}$. Use canceling to divide 4 into both 4 and 8, $\frac{9}{\overset{}{4}} \times \frac{\overset{2}{8}}{11}$. Multiply the numerators to get 18, and the denominators to get 11. You now have the improper fraction $\frac{18}{11}$. Divide 11 into 18 to get a mixed number answer of $1\frac{7}{11}$.

10. Change $2\frac{4}{5}$ to an improper fraction $\frac{14}{5}$. Now invert $\frac{14}{5}$ to its reciprocal of $\frac{5}{14}$ and change the problem to multiplication, $\frac{7}{3} \times \frac{5}{14}$. Use canceling to divide 7 into 14 and into itself, $\frac{\overset{1}{7}}{3} \times \frac{5}{\underset{2}{14}}$. Multiply the remaining numerators and denominators to get an answer of $\frac{5}{6}$.

CHAPTER FIVE

Awesome Addition

What did $\frac{1}{2}$ of a bagel say to the other $\frac{1}{2}$?

"Together we make a whole."

SAME SUPER DENOMINATOR

When you add 3 apples to 2 apples you get 5 apples. When you add 5 oranges to 3 oranges you get 8 oranges. It's the same with fractions with the same denominator. When the denominators are the same (like the same kind of fruit), keep the denominators (like the fruit *name*) and add the numerators (like the *number* of apples or oranges). Then simplify your answer by reducing or by changing to a mixed number in simplest form.

Proper fractions

For example, add the proper fractions $\frac{1}{7} + \frac{3}{7}$.

1. Keep the 7 as your denominator (like the *name* apples or oranges).

2. Add the numerators (like the *number* of apples or oranges).

3. Your answer is $\frac{4}{7}$, which is in simplest form.

Mixed number and proper fraction

For another example, add the mixed number and the fraction $2\frac{3}{5} + \frac{1}{5}$.

1. Keep the 5 as your denominator (same fruit).

2. Add the two numerators.

$$\frac{3}{5} + \frac{1}{5} = \frac{4}{5}$$

3. In this case, the whole number remains unchanged, and becomes part of your answer.

4. Your answer is $2\frac{4}{5}$.

Whole number and mixed number

Can you add a whole number to a mixed number?

Sure; for example, add $5 + 3\frac{1}{7}$.

1. Keep the fraction the same and add the two whole numbers.

$$5 + 3 = 8$$

2. Your answer is $8\frac{1}{7}$.

Can the whole number be the second number?

Absolutely; for example, add $3\frac{1}{7} + 5$.

1. Keep the fraction the same and add the two whole numbers.

$$3 + 5 = 8$$

2. Your answer is $8\frac{1}{7}$.

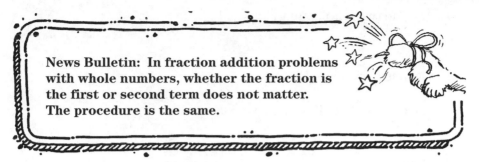

News Bulletin: In fraction addition problems with whole numbers, whether the fraction is the first or second term does not matter. The procedure is the same.

Two mixed numbers

What if you have two mixed numbers?

No problem at all. For example, add $3\frac{5}{8} + 2\frac{1}{8}$.

1. Keep the denominator the same (same fruit).

2. Add the two numerators.

$$\frac{5}{8} + \frac{1}{8} = \frac{6}{8}$$

3. Add the two whole numbers.

$$3 + 2 = 5$$

4. Your answer at this point is $5\frac{6}{8}$.

5. Reduce the fraction by dividing 6 and 8 by 2, $\frac{\cancel{6}^{3}}{\cancel{8}_{4}}$.

6. The answer is $5\frac{3}{4}$.

For another example, add $3\frac{2}{3} + 1\frac{1}{3}$.

1. Keep the denominator the same (same fruit again).

2. Add the two numerators.

$$\frac{2}{3} + \frac{1}{3} = \frac{3}{3}$$

3. Add the two whole numbers.

$$3 + 1 = 4$$

4. The answer now is $4\frac{3}{3}$.

5. Since $\frac{3}{3}$ equals 1, $4\frac{3}{3} = 4 + 1 = 5$.

What about $2\frac{3}{5} + \frac{4}{5}$?

1. Keep the 5 as your denominator (same fruit).

2. Add the two numerators.

$$\frac{3}{5} + \frac{4}{5} = \frac{7}{5}$$

3. You now have $2\frac{7}{5}$.

4. Since $\frac{7}{5}$ is an improper fraction, change it to the mixed number $1\frac{2}{5}$.

5. The problem now looks like $2 + 1\frac{2}{5}$.

6. Add the whole numbers and keep the fraction to get an answer of $3\frac{2}{5}$.

For yet another easy example, add $4\frac{2}{7} + 5\frac{6}{7}$.

1. Keep the denominator the same (same fruit once again).

2. Add the two numerators.

$$\frac{2}{7} + \frac{6}{7} = \frac{8}{7}$$

3. Add the two whole numbers.

$$4 + 5 = 9$$

4. Your answer at this point is $9\frac{8}{7}$.

5. Since $\frac{8}{7}$ equals $1\frac{1}{7}$, simplify by adding the whole numbers and bringing along the fraction.

$$9\frac{8}{7} = 9 + 1\frac{1}{7}$$

6. Your answer is $10\frac{1}{7}$.

SILLY:

$2\frac{8}{3}$ (a mixed number containing an improper fraction)

SUPERB:

$4\frac{2}{3}$ (From SILLY above, change the improper fraction $\frac{8}{3}$ to the mixed number $2\frac{2}{3}$. Then add $2 + 2\frac{2}{3}$ to get $4\frac{2}{3}$.)

DIFFERENT DELIGHTFUL DENOMINATORS

When the denominators are delightfully different (like oranges and apples), you must find a common denominator, preferably the LCD (like mixing the fruit together in a fruit salad).

Change each of the original denominators into the LCD by building equivalent fractions. Now, since the denominators are the same,

- keep the new denominator,
- add the numerators and whole numbers, and
- simplify your answer.

Proper fractions

Is it easy to work with two proper fractions that have different denominators?

Yes it is. For example, add $\frac{5}{12} + \frac{1}{3}$.

1. Find the LCM for 12 and 3 because they are different denominators (different fruit). The LCM equals 12 because 12 is the lowest number that both 3 and 12 can divide into evenly.

   (You can use a higher common denominator that both 12 and 3 divide into evenly, but you will have to reduce later.)

2. Rewrite each of the original fractions with the LCD by building an equivalent fraction for each one,

   $\frac{5}{12} = \frac{5}{12}$ and $\frac{1}{3} = \frac{4}{12}$.

3. The problem now looks like $\frac{5}{12} + \frac{4}{12}$.

4. Keep the denominator the same (now it's the same fruit).

5. Add the two numerators.

$$\frac{5}{12} + \frac{4}{12} = \frac{9}{12}$$

6. Your answer at this point is $\frac{9}{12}$.

7. Simplify your answer by dividing 9 and 12 by 3.

$$9 \div 3 = 3 \qquad \frac{\cancel{9}\,3}{\cancel{12}\,4}$$
$$12 \div 3 = 4$$

8. Your answer in lowest terms is $\frac{3}{4}$.

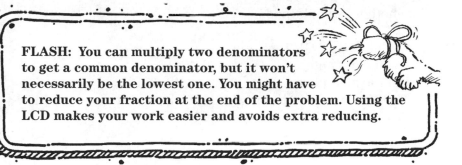

FLASH: You can multiply two denominators to get a common denominator, but it won't necessarily be the lowest one. You might have to reduce your fraction at the end of the problem. Using the LCD makes your work easier and avoids extra reducing.

Mixed numbers

What about mixed numbers, the ones with a whole number and a fraction?

For example, add $3\frac{2}{7} + 1\frac{1}{6}$.

1. Calculate the LCM for 7 and 6.
   List the multiples of 7: 7, 14, 21, 28, 35, 42, 49, 56, 63,...
   List the multiples of 6: 6, 12, 18, 24, 30, 36, 42,...
   The LCM equals 42 because 42 is the lowest common multiple that both 7 and 6 divide into evenly.

2. Rewrite each of the original fractions with the LCD by building an equivalent fraction for each one; $3\frac{2}{7} = 3\frac{12}{42}$ because $42 \div 7 = 6$ and $6 \times 2 = 12$, and $1\frac{1}{6} = 1\frac{7}{42}$ because $42 \div 6 = 7$ and $7 \times 1 = 7$.

3. The problem now looks like $3\frac{12}{42} + 1\frac{7}{42}$.

4. Keep the denominator the same.

5. Add the two numerators.

$$\frac{12}{42} + \frac{7}{42} = \frac{19}{42}$$

6. Add the two whole numbers.

$$3 + 1 = 4$$

7. Your answer is $4\frac{19}{42}$ which is in simplest form.

For another example, add $2\frac{3}{4} + 4\frac{2}{3}$.

1. Calculate the LCM for 4 and 3.
   List the multiples of 4: 4, 8, 12, 16,...
   List the multiples of 3: 3, 6, 9, 12, 15,...
   The LCM equals 12 because 12 is the lowest common multiple that both 4 and 3 divide into evenly.

2. Rewrite each of the original fractions with the LCD by building an equivalent fraction for each one; $2\frac{3}{4} = 2\frac{9}{12}$ because $12 \div 4 = 3$ and $3 \times 3 = 9$ and $4\frac{2}{3} = 4\frac{8}{12}$ because $12 \div 3 = 4$ and $4 \times 2 = 8$.

3. The problem now looks like $2\frac{9}{12} + 4\frac{8}{12}$.

4. Keep the denominator the same.

5. Add the two numerators, $\frac{9}{12} + \frac{8}{12} = \frac{17}{12}$.

6. Change $\frac{17}{12}$ to a mixed number by dividing 12 into 17 and making a fraction out of the remainder, $\frac{17}{12} = 1\frac{5}{12}$.

7. Add the whole numbers in the original problem, $2 + 4 + 1\frac{5}{12}$.

8. Your answer is $7\frac{5}{12}$, which is in simplest form.

If the denominators are relatively prime numbers, the GCF of the denominators is 1. Then, just multiply the denominators to find the LCD. For example, $\frac{1}{4} + \frac{5}{7}$ would have an LCD of 28 because $4 \times 7 = 28$.

Three or more fractions

Food for thought: You may be wondering
if three's a crowd here—not with fractions.
Two or more fractions can be added. There is
no maximum to the number of fractions that can be added.
You just need to find an LCD for *all* your denominators.

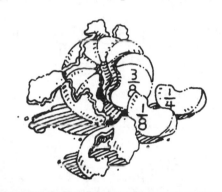

A Threesome

Add $1\frac{1}{2} + \frac{4}{5} + 2\frac{3}{4}$.

1. Find the LCM for all three denominators.
   List the multiples of 2: 2, 4, 6, 8, 10, 12, 14, 16, 18, 20, 22,...
   List the multiples of 4: 4, 8, 12, 16, 20,...
   List the multiples of 5: 5, 10, 15, 20, 25, 30,...
   The LCM is 20 because 20 is the least common multiple that 2, 4, and 5 divide into evenly.

2. Rewrite each of the original fractions with the LCD by building an equivalent fraction for each one.

   $1\frac{1}{2} = 1\frac{10}{20}$ because $20 \div 2 = 10$ and $10 \times 1 = 10$.

   $\frac{4}{5} = \frac{16}{20}$ because $20 \div 5 = 4$ and $4 \times 4 = 16$.

   $2\frac{3}{4} = 2\frac{15}{20}$ because $20 \div 4 = 5$ and $5 \times 3 = 15$.

3. The problem now looks like $1\frac{10}{20} + \frac{16}{20} + 2\frac{15}{20}$.

4. Keep the denominator the same.

5. Add the three numerators.

$$\frac{10}{20} + \frac{16}{20} + \frac{15}{20} = \frac{41}{20}$$

6. Add the two whole numbers.

$$1 + 2 = 3$$

7. Your answer at this point is $3\frac{41}{20}$, but it needs some more work.

8. Change the fractional part to a mixed number.

$$41 \div 20 = 2\frac{1}{20}$$

9. Add the $2\frac{1}{20}$ to the 3.

$$2\frac{1}{20} + 3 = 5\frac{1}{20}$$

Your answer is $5\frac{1}{20}$.

- -

If your answer is something like $5\frac{6}{6}$ or $5\frac{7}{6}$, change the fractional part to a whole number or a mixed number and simplify as for problems with the same denominator.

$$5\frac{6}{6} = 5 + 1 = 6 \qquad 5\frac{7}{6} = 5 + 1\frac{1}{6} = 6\frac{1}{6}$$

BRAIN TICKLERS
Set # 8

Add the following funtastic fractions:

1. $\frac{3}{4} + \frac{2}{9}$

2. $\frac{3}{10} + \frac{1}{6}$

3. $5 + 2\frac{3}{7}$

4. $3\frac{3}{8} + 2\frac{2}{3}$

5. $4\frac{3}{4} + 3$

6. $7\frac{8}{11} + 2\frac{2}{11}$

7. $1\frac{1}{2} + \frac{1}{4} + \frac{3}{8}$

8. $6\frac{3}{4} + \frac{1}{4}$

9. $\frac{1}{5} + \frac{7}{8} + \frac{9}{10}$

10. $7\frac{1}{2} + 6\frac{2}{3}$

(Answers are on pages 88–90.)

BRAIN TICKLERS—THE ANSWERS

Set # 8, page 87

For all of these brain ticklers, find a common denominator that all of your denominators can divide into evenly. The best common denominator is the LCM, or least common multiple.

1. List the multiples of 4: 4, 8, 12, 16, 20, 24, 28, 32, 36 . . . . List the multiples of 9: 9, 18, 27, 36 . . . . The LCM is 36. Rewrite $\frac{3}{4}$ with a denominator of 36, $\frac{3}{4} = \frac{?}{36}$. Divide 4 into 36 and multiply the result by 3 to fill in the ?, $36 \div 4 = 9$ and $9 \times 3 = 27$. So, $\frac{3}{4} = \frac{27}{36}$. Similarly, $\frac{2}{9} = \frac{8}{36}$. The problem now looks like $\frac{27}{36} + \frac{8}{36}$. Add the numerators. The answer is $\frac{35}{36}$.

2. List the multiples of 10: 10, 20, 30, 40 . . . . List the multiples of 6: 6, 12, 18, 24, 30 . . . . The LCM is 30. Rewrite $\frac{3}{10}$ with the denominator of 30, $\frac{3}{10} = \frac{?}{30}$. Divide 10 into 30 and multiply the result by 3 to fill in the ?, $30 \div 10 = 3$ and $3 \times 3 = 9$. So, $\frac{3}{10} = \frac{9}{30}$. Similarly, $\frac{1}{6} = \frac{5}{30}$. The problem now looks like $\frac{9}{30} + \frac{5}{30}$. Add the numerators to get $\frac{14}{30}$. Since 2 is a common factor to both 14 and 30, divide 2 into both the numerator and denominator, $\frac{\overset{7}{\cancel{14}}}{\underset{15}{\cancel{30}}} = \frac{7}{15}$. Your answer in simplest form is $\frac{7}{15}$.

3. In this problem, a common denominator is not necessary since 5 is a whole number. Add the two whole numbers, $5 + 2 = 7$, and bring along the fraction. Your answer is $7\frac{3}{7}$.

4. List the multiples of 8: 8, 16, 24 . . . . List the multiples of 3: 3, 6, 9, 12, 15, 18, 21, 24 . . . . The LCM is 24. Rewrite $\frac{3}{8}$ with a denominator of 24, $\frac{3}{8} = \frac{?}{24}$. Divide 8 into 24 and multiply the result by 3 to fill in the ?, $24 \div 8 = 3$ and $3 \times 3 = 9$. So, $\frac{3}{8} = \frac{9}{24}$. Similarly, $\frac{2}{3} = \frac{16}{24}$. The problem now looks like $3\frac{9}{24} + 2\frac{16}{24}$. Add the whole numbers, $3 + 2 = 5$, and your fractions $\frac{9}{24} + \frac{16}{24} = \frac{25}{24}$. You now have $5\frac{25}{24}$. Change the $\frac{25}{24}$ to a mixed number by dividing 24 into 25 to get $1\frac{1}{24}$. You now have $5 + 1\frac{1}{24}$. Add the two whole numbers and bring along the fraction to get an answer of $6\frac{1}{24}$.

5. Here, a common denominator is unnecessary. Simply add the two whole numbers and bring along the fraction, $4\frac{3}{4} + 3 - 7\frac{3}{4}$.

6. Since the denominators are the same, you can keep this denominator and add the two numerators, $\frac{8}{11} + \frac{2}{11} = \frac{10}{11}$. Then add the two whole numbers, $7 + 2 = 9$. Your answer is $9\frac{10}{11}$.

7. Here you have three different denominators, so list the multiples for each one. The multiples of 2 are 2, 4, 6, 8 . . . , the multiples of 4 are 4, 8, 12 . . . , and the multiples of 8 are 8, 16 . . . . The LCM for all three is 8. Rewrite $\frac{1}{2}$ with a denominator of 8, $\frac{1}{2} = \frac{?}{8}$. Divide 2 into 8 and multiply the result by 1 to fill in the ?, $8 \div 2 = 4$ and $4 \times 1 = 4$. So, $\frac{1}{2} = \frac{4}{8}$. Similarly, $\frac{1}{4} = \frac{2}{8}$. The fraction $\frac{3}{8}$ stays the same because the denominator is already 8. The problem now looks like $1\frac{4}{8} + \frac{2}{8} + \frac{3}{8}$. Since there is only one whole number, add the numerators of the fractions and bring along the whole number to get $1\frac{9}{8}$.

Now change $\frac{9}{8}$ to a mixed number by dividing 8 into 9 to get $1\frac{1}{8}$. You now have $1 + 1\frac{1}{8}$. Add the two whole numbers and bring along the fraction to get an answer of $2\frac{1}{8}$.

8. Since the denominators are the same, keep this denominator and add the two numerators, $\frac{3}{4} + \frac{1}{4} = \frac{4}{4}$. Since $\frac{4}{4} = 1$, add this 1 to the whole number 6. Your answer is 7.

9. List the multiples for each of the three denominators. The multiples of 5 are 5, 10, 15, 20, 25, 30, 35, 40 . . . , the multiples of 8 are 8, 16, 24, 32, 40 . . . , and the multiples of 10 are 10, 20, 30, 40 . . . . The LCM is 40. Rewrite $\frac{1}{5}$ with a denominator of 40, $\frac{1}{5} = \frac{?}{40}$. Divide 5 into 40 and multiply the result by 1 to fill in the ?, $40 \div 5 = 8$ and $8 \times 1 = 8$. So, $\frac{1}{5} = \frac{8}{40}$. Similarly, $\frac{7}{8} = \frac{35}{40}$, and $\frac{9}{10} = \frac{36}{40}$. The problem now reads $\frac{8}{40} + \frac{35}{40} + \frac{36}{40}$. Add the numerators to equal $\frac{79}{40}$. Change $\frac{79}{40}$ to a mixed number by dividing 40 into 79 to get an answer of $1\frac{39}{40}$.

10. List the multiples of 2: 2, 4, 6, 8 . . . . List the multiples of 3: 3, 6, 9, 12 . . . . Here, 6 is the LCM. Rewrite $\frac{1}{2}$ with a denominator of 6, $\frac{1}{2} = \frac{?}{6}$. Divide 2 into 6 and multiply the result by 1 to fill in the ?, $6 \div 2 = 3$ and $3 \times 1 = 3$. So, $\frac{1}{2} = \frac{3}{6}$. Similarly, $\frac{2}{3} = \frac{4}{6}$. The problem now reads $7\frac{3}{6} + 6\frac{4}{6}$. Add the whole numbers, $7 + 6 = 13$, and the fractions, $\frac{3}{6} + \frac{4}{6} = \frac{7}{6}$. You now have $13\frac{7}{6}$. Rewrite $\frac{7}{6}$ as the mixed number $1\frac{1}{6}$. The problem now reads $13 + 1\frac{1}{6}$. Add the two whole numbers and bring along the fraction to get an answer of $14\frac{1}{6}$.

CHAPTER SIX

Sparkling Subtraction

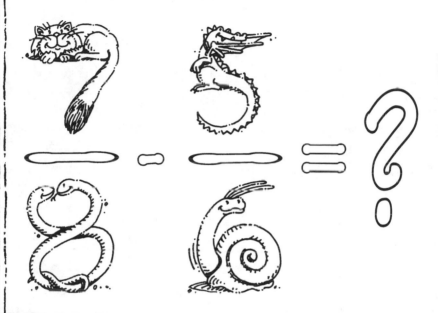

To be a fraction master,

Requires quite a feat;

If you can do subtraction,

You'll be on easy street.

For most subtraction problems, the procedure is the same as that for adding fractions except that you *subtract* the numerators instead of *add* them.

SAME SUPER DENOMINATOR

For the **same denominator** (all apples *or* all oranges), keep the denominator and subtract the numerators and the whole numbers.

$$\frac{4}{7} - \frac{2}{7} = \frac{2}{7} \qquad\qquad 4\frac{4}{7} - 3\frac{1}{7} = 1\frac{3}{7}$$

DIFFERENT DELIGHTFUL DENOMINATORS

For **different denominators** (both apples *and* oranges), calculate a common denominator (the LCM—the fruit salad). Change each of the original denominators into the LCM by building equivalent fractions. Now, since the denominators are the same,

- keep the new denominator,
- subtract the numerators and whole numbers, and
- simplify your answer.

Subtract $\frac{6}{9} - \frac{1}{4}$.

1. Find the LCM of 9 and 4.
   List the multiples of 9:   9, 18, 27, 36,…
   List the multiples of 4:   4, 8, 12, 16, 20, 24, 28, 32, 36,…
   The LCM equals 36 because 36 is the lowest number that both 9 and 4 can divide into evenly.

2. Rewrite each of the original fractions with the LCD by building an equivalent fraction for each one; $\frac{6}{9} = \frac{24}{36}$ by dividing 36 by 9 and multiplying the result by 6.

$$36 \div 9 = 4 \qquad\qquad 4 \times 6 = 24$$

   Also, $\frac{1}{4} = \frac{9}{36}$ by dividing 36 by 4 and multiplying the result by 1.

$$36 \div 4 = 9 \qquad\qquad 9 \times 1 = 9$$

3. The problem now looks like $\frac{24}{36} - \frac{9}{36}$.

4. Keep the denominator the same.

5. Subtract the two numerators.

$$24 - 9 = 15$$

6. Your answer at this point is $\frac{15}{36}$.

7. Reduce your answer (by dividing 15 and 36 by 3) to equal $\frac{5}{12}$, which is in simplest form.

Another Spectacular Example

Subtract $12\frac{5}{12} - 3\frac{1}{4}$.

1. Find the LCM of 12 and 4.
   List the multiples of 12: 12, 24, 36,...
   List the multiples of 4: 4, 8, 12, 16,...
   The LCM equals 12 because 12 is the lowest number that both 12 and 4 can divide into evenly.

2. Rewrite each of the original fractions with the LCD by building an equivalent fraction for each one: $12\frac{5}{12} = 12\frac{5}{12}$ because 12 is already the LCD, and $3\frac{1}{4} = 3\frac{3}{12}$ because $12 \div 4 = 3$ and $3 \times 1 = 3$.

3. The problem now looks like $12\frac{5}{12} - 3\frac{3}{12}$.

4. Keep the denominator the same.

5. Subtract the two numerators.
$$\frac{5}{12} - \frac{3}{12} = \frac{2}{12}$$

6. Subtract the two whole numbers.
$$12 - 3 = 9$$

7. Your answer at this point is $9\frac{2}{12}$.

8. Reduce the fraction by dividing 2 and 12 by 2.
$$\frac{2 \div 2}{12 \div 2} = \frac{1}{6}$$

9. Your answer is $9\frac{1}{6}$.

MIXED NUMBER AND WHOLE NUMBER (WITHOUT BORROWING)

Mixing bowl #1

The mixed number is first and the whole number is second. For example, subtract $8\frac{1}{2} - 3$.

1. When the fraction is in the first number, you can just bring it down to your answer.

2. Subtract the whole numbers.

$$8 - 3 = 5$$

3. Your answer is $5\frac{1}{2}$.

Borrowing is a process where you subtract 1 whole from a number, and you trade the 1 that you subtracted for a fraction equal to 1. This fraction depends on the denominator of the original problem.

MIXED NUMBER AND WHOLE NUMBER (WITH BORROWING)

Mixing bowl #2—Switch the ingredients

The whole number is first and the mixed number is second.

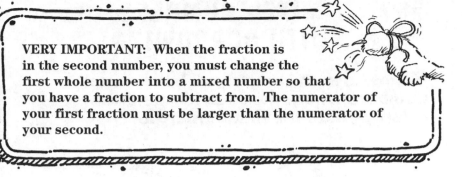

VERY IMPORTANT: When the fraction is in the second number, you must change the first whole number into a mixed number so that you have a fraction to subtract from. The numerator of your first fraction must be larger than the numerator of your second.

For example, subtract $8 - 6\frac{1}{2}$.

1. Use borrowing to subtract 1 whole from the number 8, making it a 7.

2. Trade the 1 that you subtracted for a fraction with the same numerator and denominator as the denominator in the original problem, in this case, $\frac{2}{2}$.

3. Now, $8 = 7\frac{2}{2}$.

4. The problem now looks like $7\frac{2}{2} - 6\frac{1}{2}$.

5. Now proceed to subtract the whole numbers and the fractions, $7 - 6 = 1$ and $\frac{2}{2} - \frac{1}{2} = \frac{1}{2}$. Your answer is $1\frac{1}{2}$.

RIGHT MIX:

$6\frac{1}{3} - 4 = 2\frac{1}{3}$

MESSED-UP MIX:

$6 - 4\frac{1}{3} = 2\frac{1}{3}$

RIGHT MIX:

$6 - 4\frac{1}{3} = 5\frac{3}{3} - 4\frac{1}{3} = 1\frac{2}{3}$

MIXED NUMBERS (WITH BORROWING)

What happens when you have mixed numbers where the second numerator is larger than the first numerator?

Let's try one where the denominators are the same.

For example (same fruit again), subtract $3\frac{1}{5} - 2\frac{4}{5}$.

You must trade or borrow here, too, but in a slightly different way from the previous problem.

Change the first mixed number into an equivalent form where the first fraction will be larger than the second fraction.

1. As before, subtract 1 whole from the first number, 3, making it a 2.

2. Trade the whole that you subtracted for a fraction with the same numerator and denominator as the denominator in the original problem, or $\frac{5}{5}$ in this case.

3. Now, $3 = 2\frac{5}{5}$.

4. Add this $\frac{5}{5}$ to the $\frac{1}{5}$ that is already there.

5. The first fraction now looks like $3\frac{1}{5} = 2\frac{5}{5} + \frac{1}{5} = 2\frac{6}{5}$.

6. The second fraction, $2\frac{4}{5}$, stays the same.

7. The problem now looks like $2\frac{6}{5} - 2\frac{4}{5}$.

8. Now subtract the whole number and the fractions.

$$2 - 2 = 0 \qquad\qquad \frac{6}{5} - \frac{4}{5} = \frac{2}{5}$$

9. Your answer is $\frac{2}{5}$.

Alternate Method

$3\frac{1}{5} - 2\frac{4}{5}$

1. Change both of the mixed numbers into improper fractions:
    $3\frac{1}{5} = \frac{16}{5}$ and $2\frac{4}{5} = \frac{14}{5}$.

2. Subtract $\frac{16}{5} - \frac{14}{5}$.

3. The answer is $\frac{2}{5}$.

Now let's try one where the denominators are different. First select a common denominator.

For example, subtract $8\frac{1}{5} - 4\frac{3}{10}$.

1. Change the denominators into a common one.
   List the multiples of 5: 5, 10, 15,...
   List the multiples of 10: 10, 20,...
   The LCD, the least common denominator, equals 10 because 10 is the lowest number that both 5 and 10 can divide into evenly.

2. Rewrite each of the original fractions with the LCD:
   $8\frac{1}{5} = 8\frac{2}{10}$, by dividing 5 into 10 and multiplying the result by 1, and $4\frac{3}{10} = 4\frac{3}{10}$ because 10 is already the LCD.

3. Then you will notice that the second fraction is larger than the first, $8\frac{2}{10} - 4\frac{3}{10}$. So you must borrow.

4. With $8\frac{2}{10}$, subtract 1 from the 8 making it a 7.

5. Trade the 1 that you subtracted for a fraction with the same numerator and denominator as the denominator in the original problem. This 1 is equal to $\frac{10}{10}$. Now $8 = 7\frac{10}{10}$.

6. Add this $\frac{10}{10}$ to the $\frac{2}{10}$ which is already there. $8\frac{2}{10} = 7\frac{10}{10} + \frac{2}{10} = 7\frac{12}{10}$.

7. The problem now looks like $7\frac{12}{10} - 4\frac{3}{10}$.

8. Subtract the numerators, $\frac{12}{10} - \frac{3}{10} = \frac{9}{10}$, and keep the denominators the same.

9. Subtract the whole numbers, $7 - 4 = 3$, and your answer is $3\frac{9}{10}$.

Here is another example requiring borrowing: $6\frac{2}{3} - 3\frac{7}{8}$.

1. Change the denominators into a common one.
   List the multiples of 3: 3, 6, 9, 12, 15, 18, 21, 24,...
   List the multiples of 8: 8, 16, 24,...
The LCM is 24 because 24 is the lowest number that both 3 and 8 can divide into evenly.

2. Rewrite each of the original fractions with the least common denominator: $6\frac{2}{3} = 6\frac{16}{24}$ by dividing 3 into 24 and multiplying the result by 2. Similarly, $3\frac{7}{8} = 3\frac{21}{24}$ by dividing 8 into 24 and multiplying the result by 7.

3. Then you will notice that the second fraction is larger than the first, $6\frac{16}{24} - 3\frac{21}{24}$. So you must borrow.

4. With $6\frac{16}{24}$ subtract 1 from the 6 making it a 5.

5. Trade the 1 that you subtracted for a fraction with the common denominator of 24. This 1 would equal $\frac{24}{24}$. Now, $6 = 5\frac{24}{24}$.

6. Add this $5\frac{24}{24}$ to the $\frac{16}{24}$ which is already there.
$6\frac{16}{24} = 5\frac{24}{24} + \frac{16}{24} = 5\frac{40}{24}$.

7. The problem now looks like $5\frac{40}{24} - 3\frac{21}{24}$.

8. Subtract the numerators, $\frac{40}{24} - \frac{21}{24} = \frac{19}{24}$, and keep the denominators the same.

9. Subtract the whole numbers, $5 - 3 = 2$, and your answer is $2\frac{19}{24}$.

Alternate Method

$8\frac{1}{5} - 4\frac{3}{10}$

1. Change both of the mixed numbers into improper fractions, $8\frac{1}{5} = \frac{41}{5}$ and $4\frac{3}{10} = \frac{43}{10}$.

2. The problem now looks like $\frac{41}{5} - \frac{43}{10}$.

3. Find an LCM for 5 and 10.
List the multiples of 5:   5, 10, 15, 20,…
List the multiples of 10:   10, 20, 30,…
The LCD, the least common denominator, equals 10 because 10 is the lowest number that both 5 and 10 can divide into evenly.

4. Rewrite $\frac{41}{5}$ with the common denominator: $\frac{41}{5} = \frac{82}{10}$, by dividing 5 into 10 and multiplying the result by 41. $\frac{43}{10}$ already has 10 as the lowest common denominator.

5. The problem now looks like $\frac{82}{10} - \frac{43}{10}$.

6. Subtract the numerators and keep the denominators the same, $\frac{82}{10} - \frac{43}{10} = \frac{39}{10}$.

7. Simplify $\frac{39}{10}$ by changing it to a mixed number of $3\frac{9}{10}$.

• •

ADDITION-SUBTRACTION COMBO

Now, let's try a *SUPER DUPER* combination addition-subtraction problem.

For example, $\frac{7}{8} + \frac{1}{4} - \frac{1}{2}$.

1. Change the denominators into the common one.
   List the multiples of 8: 8, 16,…
   List the multiples of 4: 4, 8, 12,…
   List the multiples of 2: 2, 4, 6, 8,…
   The LCM is 8 because 8 is the lowest number that 2, 4, and 8 can divide into evenly.

2. Rewrite each of the original fractions with the new common denominator.

   $\frac{7}{8} = \frac{7}{8}$ because 8 is already the common denominator.

   $\frac{1}{4} = \frac{2}{8}$ because $8 \div 4 = 2$ and $2 \times 1 = 2$.

   $\frac{1}{2} = \frac{4}{8}$ because $8 \div 2 = 4$ and $4 \times 1 = 4$.

3. The problem now looks like $\frac{7}{8} + \frac{2}{8} - \frac{4}{8}$.

4. Since the denominators are the same, add your two numerators $\frac{7}{8} + \frac{2}{8} = \frac{9}{8}$ and subtract the other numerator, $\frac{9}{8} - \frac{4}{8} = \frac{5}{8}$. The final answer is $\frac{5}{8}$.

BRAIN TICKLERS
Set # 9

Subtract the following funtastic fractions:

1. $\frac{4}{9} - \frac{2}{9}$

2. $7\frac{3}{7} - 4$

3. $3\frac{2}{5} - 2\frac{1}{8}$

4. $8 - 5\frac{3}{5}$

5. $11\frac{3}{7} - 8\frac{5}{7}$

6. $6\frac{1}{2} - 2\frac{7}{10}$

7. $9 - 7\frac{8}{9}$

8. $4\frac{1}{5} - 3\frac{3}{4}$

9. $16\frac{3}{8} - 8\frac{1}{4}$

10. $\frac{7}{10} - \frac{1}{2} + \frac{1}{5}$

11. $5\frac{1}{5} - 2\frac{2}{3}$

12. $10\frac{3}{4} - \frac{5}{6}$

(Answers are on pages 104–108.)

BRAIN TICKLERS—THE ANSWERS

Set # 9, page 103

1. Since both fractions have the same denominator, simply subtract the two numerators, $\frac{4}{9} - \frac{2}{9} = \frac{4-2}{9}$ to get an answer of $\frac{2}{9}$.

2. Here, since the fraction is in the first part of the problem, you can subtract the two whole numbers and simply bring the fraction along to the answer, $7\frac{3}{7} - 4 = 3\frac{3}{7}$.

3. In order to subtract, you must find a common denominator for 5 and 8. List the multiples of 5: 5, 10, 15, 20, 25, 30, 35, 40, 45 . . . . List the multiples of 8: 8, 16, 24, 32, 40, 48 . . . . The LCM, the common denominator, is 40. Rewrite $\frac{2}{5}$ with the new denominator of 40, $\frac{2}{5} = \frac{?}{40}$. Divide 5 into 40 and multiply the result by 2. Because $40 \div 5 = 8$ and $8 \times 2 = 16$, $\frac{2}{5} = \frac{16}{40}$. Similarly, $\frac{1}{8} = \frac{5}{40}$ because $40 \div 8 = 5$ and $5 \times 1 = 5$. You now have $3\frac{16}{40} - 2\frac{5}{40}$. Since the denominators are now the same, and the first fraction is larger than the second, you just subtract the whole numbers and the fractions to get the answer of $1\frac{11}{40}$.

4. To complete the subtraction, you must change the 8 into a mixed number with 5 as the denominator of the fraction in order to match the other denominator of 5 already in the problem. To do this, subtract 1 from the number 8 making it a 7. This 1 that you subtracted or traded is equal to $\frac{5}{5}$. So, $8 = 7\frac{5}{5}$. The problem now looks like $7\frac{5}{5} - 5\frac{3}{5}$. Now, subtract the whole numbers and fractions to get the answer of $2\frac{2}{5}$.

5. Since the denominators are the same, you do not have to find a new common denominator. However, you cannot subtract the larger fraction of $\frac{5}{7}$ from the smaller fraction of $\frac{3}{7}$ in this form. You must change $11\frac{3}{7}$ to an equivalent mixed number so that it contains a fraction larger than $\frac{5}{7}$. To do this, subtract 1 whole from the 11, making it a 10. The 1 whole that you borrowed is equal to $\frac{7}{7}$ in this problem because of the 7 that is the denominator in the original problem. Add this $\frac{7}{7}$ to the $\frac{3}{7}$ that is already there, $11\frac{3}{7} = 10\frac{7}{7} + \frac{3}{7} = 10\frac{10}{7}$. Now the problem looks like $10\frac{10}{7} - 8\frac{5}{7}$. Subtract the whole numbers and the fractions. The answer is $2\frac{5}{7}$.

6. Find a common denominator for 2 and 10. The multiples of 2 are 2, 4, 6, 8, 10 . . . , and the multiples of 10 are 10, 20, 30 . . . . The LCM, which is the lowest common denominator, is 10. Rewrite $\frac{1}{2}$ with the new common denominator of 10, $\frac{1}{2} = \frac{?}{10}$. Because $10 \div 2 = 5$ and $5 \times 1 = 5$, the ? is equal to 5. So, $\frac{1}{2} = \frac{5}{10}$. The fraction $\frac{7}{10}$ is already written with the common denominator. The problem now looks like $6\frac{5}{10} - 2\frac{7}{10}$. Now you must rewrite $6\frac{5}{10}$ as an equivalent mixed number so that its fraction will be larger than $\frac{7}{10}$. Subtract 1 whole from the 6, making it a 5. The 1 whole that you subtracted can be traded for $\frac{10}{10}$, as $1 = \frac{10}{10}$. Add $\frac{10}{10}$ to the $\frac{5}{10}$ that is already there, $6\frac{5}{10} = 5\frac{10}{10} + \frac{5}{10} = 5\frac{15}{10}$. Now the problem looks like $5\frac{15}{10} - 2\frac{7}{10}$. Subtract the two whole numbers and the fractions to get an answer of $3\frac{8}{10}$. The fraction $\frac{8}{10}$ can be reduced to $\frac{4}{5}$ by dividing both the numerator and denominator by the common factor of 2, $\frac{\cancel{8}^{4}}{\cancel{10}_{5}}$. Your simplified answer is $3\frac{4}{5}$.

7. To complete the subtraction, you must change the 9 into a mixed number with 9 as the denominator of the fraction in order to match the other denominator of 9 already in the problem. To do this, subtract 1 whole from the 9, making it an 8. This 1 whole that you subtracted or traded is equal to $\frac{9}{9}$. So, $9 = 8\frac{9}{9}$, and $7\frac{8}{9}$ stays the same. Now subtract the two whole numbers and the two fractions, $8\frac{9}{9} - 7\frac{8}{9} = 1\frac{1}{9}$. Your answer is $1\frac{1}{9}$.

8. Find the lowest common denominator for 5 and 4. The multiples of 5 are 5, 10, 15, 20 . . . , and the multiples of 4 are 4, 8, 12, 16, 20 . . . . The LCM is 20. Rewrite $\frac{1}{5}$ with the new common denominator of 20, $\frac{1}{5} = \frac{?}{20}$. Because $20 \div 5 = 4$ and $4 \times 1 = 4$, the ? is equal to 4. So, $\frac{1}{5} = \frac{4}{20}$. Similarly, $\frac{3}{4} = \frac{?}{20}$. Because $20 \div 4 = 5$ and $5 \times 3 = 15$, the ? is equal to 15. So $\frac{3}{4} = \frac{15}{20}$. The problem now reads $4\frac{4}{20} - 3\frac{15}{20}$. Since the second numerator is larger than the first numerator, use borrowing to subtract 1 from the 4, making it a 3. Trade the 1 that you borrowed for $\frac{20}{20}$ since 20 is the common denominator. Add this $\frac{20}{20}$ to the $\frac{4}{20}$ which is already there. $4\frac{4}{20} = 3\frac{20}{20} + \frac{4}{20} = 3\frac{24}{20}$. The problem now looks like $3\frac{24}{20} - 3\frac{15}{20}$. Subtract the two whole numbers and the two numerators to get $\frac{9}{20}$.

9. Here you need a common denominator for 8 and 4. The multiples of 8 are 8, 16, 24 . . . , and the multiples of 4 are 4, 8, 12 . . . . The LCM, the common denominator, is 8. Rewrite $\frac{1}{4}$ with the common denominator of 8, $\frac{1}{4} = \frac{?}{8}$. Divide 4 into 8 and multiply the result by 1. Because $8 \div 4 = 2$ and $2 \times 1 = 2$, $\frac{1}{4} = \frac{2}{8}$. The fraction $\frac{3}{8}$ stays the same because it is already written with the common denominator. The problem now looks like $16\frac{3}{8} - 8\frac{2}{8}$. Subtract the two whole numbers and the two fractions to get the answer of $8\frac{1}{8}$.

10. Although this problem has both addition and subtraction, one common denominator will cover all three fractions. The multiples of 10 are 10, 20 . . . , the multiples of 2 are 2, 4, 6, 8, 10 . . . , and the multiples of 5 are 5, 10, 15 . . . . The LCM, the common denominator, is 10. Rewrite $\frac{1}{2}$ with the new common denominator of 10, $\frac{1}{2} = \frac{?}{10}$. Divide 2 into 10 and multiply the result by 1 to get $\frac{1}{2} = \frac{5}{10}$. Similarly, $\frac{1}{5} = \frac{2}{10}$. The fraction $\frac{7}{10}$ stays the same because it already is written with the common denominator of 10. The problem now looks like $\frac{7}{10} - \frac{5}{10} + \frac{2}{10}$. Subtract the first two numerators, $7 - 5 = 2$, and then add the third numerator, $2 + 2 = 4$. Keep the denominator of 10. Your answer so far is $\frac{4}{10}$. Reduce $\frac{4}{10}$ by dividing the common factor of 2 into both the numerator and denominator, $\frac{\cancel{4}^2}{\cancel{10}_5}$. Your final answer in simplest form is $\frac{2}{5}$.

11. Find a common denominator for 5 and 3. The multiples of 5 are 5, 10, 15, 20, 25 . . . , and the multiples of 3 are 3, 6, 9, 12, 15, 18 . . . . The LCM is 15 because 15 is the lowest number that both 5 and 3 can divide into evenly. Rewrite $\frac{1}{5}$ with the new denominator of 15, $\frac{1}{5} = \frac{?}{15}$. Divide 5 into 15 and multiply the result of 3 by 1, so that $\frac{1}{5} = \frac{3}{15}$. Similarly, $\frac{2}{3} = \frac{10}{15}$ because 15 divided by 3 equals 5 and 5 multiplied by 2 equals 10. You now have $5\frac{3}{15} - 2\frac{10}{15}$. Since the denominators are now the same, but the second numerator is larger, you must borrow in order to complete the subtraction. Subtract 1 from 5 making it 4. Now, trade the 1 that you borrowed for $\frac{15}{15}$ since 15 is the common denominator. Add this $\frac{15}{15}$ to the $\frac{3}{15}$ which is already there. $4\frac{15}{15} + \frac{3}{15} = 4\frac{18}{15}$. The problem now looks like $4\frac{18}{15} - 2\frac{10}{15}$. Subtract the two whole numbers and the two numerators to get $2\frac{8}{15}$.

12. Find a common denominator for 4 and 6. The multiples of 4 are 4, 8, 12, 16, 20 . . . , and the multiples of 6 are 6, 12, 18, 24 . . . . The LCM is 12 because 12 is the lowest number that both 4 and 6 can divide into evenly. Rewrite $\frac{3}{4}$ with the new denominator of 12, $\frac{3}{4} = \frac{?}{12}$. Divide 4 into 12 and multiply the result of 3 by 3 to get 9. So, $\frac{3}{4} = \frac{9}{12}$. Similarly, $\frac{5}{6} = \frac{10}{12}$ because 12 divided by 6 equals 2 and 2 multiplied by 5 equals 10. You now have $10\frac{9}{12} - \frac{10}{12}$. Since the second numerator is larger, you must borrow to complete the subtraction. Subtract 1 from 10 making it a 9. Now, trade the 1 you borrowed for $\frac{12}{12}$ since 12 is the common denominator. Add this $\frac{12}{12}$ to the $\frac{9}{12}$ that is already there. $9\frac{12}{12} + \frac{9}{12} = 9\frac{21}{12}$. The problem now looks like $9\frac{21}{12} - \frac{10}{12}$. Keep the 9 as the whole number and subtract the two numerators to get $9\frac{11}{12}$.

CHAPTER SEVEN

Exceptional Exponents

What did one exponent say to the other?

"Boy, we little numbers are power-ful!"

STRATEGY AND SAMPLES

An **exponent** is a little raised number to the right of another number, called the **base**. For example, in 2^3, 2 is the base and 3 is the exponent. The exponent tells how many times to multiply the base by itself. The 3 tells you how many times to multiply the 2 by itself. Therefore $2^3 = 2 \times 2 \times 2$, which equals 8. When whole numbers greater than 1 are raised to positive exponents greater than 1, the answer is a bigger number than the original base. When 1 is raised to any positive exponent, the answer is still 1. $1^2 = 1$, and also, $1^{35} = 1$. When the exponent equals 1, the answer equals the base number: $8^1 = 8$.

Caution—Major Mistake Territory!

Do not say 2^3 equals 2 times 3, which equals 6.

You can use exponents with fractions. For example, in $\left(\frac{1}{2}\right)^2$, $\frac{1}{2}$ is the base and 2 is the exponent.

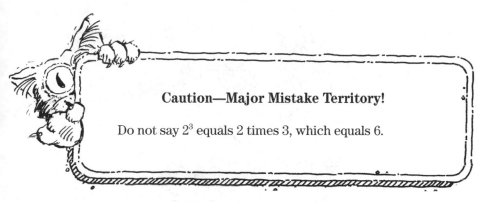

Parentheses are used here to separate the fraction from the exponent. The 2 tells you how many times to multiply the $\frac{1}{2}$ by itself. Therefore, $\left(\frac{1}{2}\right)^2$ looks like $\frac{1}{2} \cdot \frac{1}{2}$, which equals $\frac{1}{4}$. When proper fractions are raised to positive exponents greater than 1, the answer is a smaller number than the original base. When improper fractions or mixed numbers are raised to positive exponents greater than 1, the answer is a larger number than the original base.

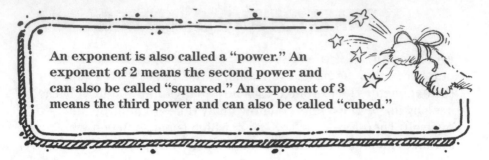

An exponent is also called a "power." An exponent of 2 means the second power and can also be called "squared." An exponent of 3 means the third power and can also be called "cubed."

If you have two or more fractions, you can find powers two ways. For example, in $\left(\frac{1}{3}\right)^3 \cdot \left(\frac{3}{5}\right)^2$, you can use:

Marvelous Method 1

Multiply $\left(\frac{1}{3}\right)^3 \cdot \left(\frac{3}{5}\right)^2$.

1. Use the exponents to simplify each part of the problem separately.

$$\left(\frac{1}{3}\right)^3 = \frac{1}{3} \cdot \frac{1}{3} \cdot \frac{1}{3} = \frac{1}{27} \text{ and } \left(\frac{3}{5}\right)^2 = \frac{3}{5} \cdot \frac{3}{5} = \frac{9}{25}$$

2. Multiply $\frac{1}{27}$ and $\frac{9}{25}$.

3. Use canceling to divide both the 9 and 27 by 9, since 9 is a common factor.

$$\frac{1}{3\overline{27}} \cdot \frac{\cancel{9}^{\,1}}{25}$$

4. The problem now looks like $\frac{1}{3} \cdot \frac{1}{25}$, which is equal to $\frac{1}{75}$ by multiplying the numerators and denominators.

• •

Or you can use:

Marvelous Method 2

Multiply $\left(\frac{1}{3}\right)^3 \cdot \left(\frac{3}{5}\right)^2$.

1. Use exponents to expand your problem, but don't simplify at this point. (You can work with smaller numbers this way.)

$$\left(\frac{1}{3}\right)^3 = \frac{1}{3} \cdot \frac{1}{3} \cdot \frac{1}{3} \text{ and } \left(\frac{3}{5}\right)^2 = \frac{3}{5} \cdot \frac{3}{5}$$

2. The problem looks like $\frac{1}{3} \cdot \frac{1}{3} \cdot \frac{1}{3} \cdot \frac{3}{5} \cdot \frac{3}{5}$.

3. While keeping the fractions in this form, use canceling to simplify your answer. Cancel the two 3s from the numerator with two of the 3s from the denominator.

$$\frac{1}{1\cancel{3}} \cdot \frac{1}{1\cancel{3}} \cdot \frac{1}{3} \cdot \frac{\cancel{3}^1}{5} \cdot \frac{\cancel{3}^1}{5}$$

4. The problem now looks like $\frac{1}{1} \cdot \frac{1}{1} \cdot \frac{1}{3} \cdot \frac{1}{5} \cdot \frac{1}{5}$, which is equal to $\frac{1}{75}$ by multiplying the numerators and denominators.

BRAIN TICKLERS
Set # 10

Use exponents to simplify these funtastic fractions:

1. $\left(\dfrac{1}{4}\right)^2$

2. $\left(\dfrac{2}{3}\right)^3$

3. $\left(\dfrac{1}{2}\right)^4$

4. $\left(\dfrac{1}{6}\right)^2\left(\dfrac{2}{3}\right)$

5. $\left(\dfrac{3}{7}\right)^3(7)\left(\dfrac{7}{8}\right)^2$

6. $\left(\dfrac{1}{5}\right)^4\left(\dfrac{5}{9}\right)^2$

7. $\left(\dfrac{2}{5}\right)^3(0)\left(\dfrac{5}{6}\right)$

8. $\left(\dfrac{3}{8}\right)^3(2)$

9. $\left(\dfrac{2}{3}\right)^3\left(\dfrac{1}{2}\right)^4\left(\dfrac{6}{11}\right)$

10. $(10)^0\left(\dfrac{2}{5}\right)^2$

(Answers are on pages 116–118.)

BRAIN TICKLERS—THE ANSWERS

Set # 10, page 115

Most of the solutions here use MARVELOUS METHOD 2 (see page 114), but MARVELOUS METHOD 1 (see page 113) can be used as an alternative.

1. $\left(\frac{1}{4}\right)^2$ means to multiply $\frac{1}{4} \times \frac{1}{4}$. Multiply the two numerators and the two denominators to equal $\frac{1}{16}$.

2. $\left(\frac{2}{3}\right)^3$ means to multiply $\frac{2}{3} \times \frac{2}{3} \times \frac{2}{3}$. Multiply the numerators and the denominators, $\frac{2 \times 2 \times 2}{3 \times 3 \times 3}$, to equal $\frac{8}{27}$. A shortcut for doing this problem is $\left(\frac{2}{3}\right)^3 = \frac{2^3}{3^3} = \frac{8}{27}$.

3. $\left(\frac{1}{2}\right)^4$ means to multiply $\frac{1}{2} \times \frac{1}{2} \times \frac{1}{2} \times \frac{1}{2}$. Multiply the numerators and the denominators, $\frac{1 \times 1 \times 1 \times 1}{2 \times 2 \times 2 \times 2} = \frac{1}{16}$. A shortcut for doing this problem is $\left(\frac{1}{2}\right)^4 = \frac{1^4}{2^4} = \frac{1}{16}$.

4. Expand $\left(\frac{1}{6}\right)^2\left(\frac{2}{3}\right)$ to equal $\frac{1}{6} \cdot \frac{1}{6} \cdot \frac{2}{3}$. Since there is a common factor of 2 that divides evenly into the 2 in the numerator and one of the 6s in the denominator, you can use canceling to simplify, $\frac{1}{6} \cdot \frac{1}{{}_{3}6} \cdot \frac{{}^{1}2}{3}$. Multiply the remaining numerators and denominators to equal $\frac{1}{54}$.

5. Expand $\left(\frac{3}{7}\right)^3 (7)\left(\frac{7}{8}\right)^2$ to equal $\left(\frac{3}{7}\right)^3\left(\frac{7}{1}\right)\left(\frac{7}{8}\right)^2$, then expand that to equal $\frac{3}{7} \cdot \frac{3}{7} \cdot \frac{3}{7} \cdot \frac{7}{1} \cdot \frac{7}{8} \cdot \frac{7}{8}$. Cancel the three 7s in the numerator with the three 7s in the denominator, $\frac{3}{{}_{1}7} \cdot \frac{3}{{}_{1}7} \cdot \frac{3}{{}_{1}7} \cdot \frac{{}^{1}7}{1} \cdot \frac{{}^{1}7}{8} \cdot \frac{{}^{1}7}{8}$. Multiply the remaining numerators and denominators, $\frac{3 \times 3 \times 3}{8 \times 8}$, to equal $\frac{27}{64}$.

6. Expand $\left(\frac{1}{5}\right)^4\left(\frac{5}{9}\right)^2$ to $\frac{1}{5}\cdot\frac{1}{5}\cdot\frac{1}{5}\cdot\frac{1}{5}\cdot\frac{5}{9}\cdot\frac{5}{9}$. Cancel the two 5s in the numerator with two of the 5s in the denominator, $\frac{1}{1\cancel{5}}\cdot\frac{1}{1\cancel{5}}\cdot\frac{1}{5}\cdot\frac{1}{5}\cdot\frac{\cancel{5}^1}{9}\cdot\frac{\cancel{5}^1}{9}$. Multiply the remaining numerators and denominators, $\frac{1\cdot1\cdot1\cdot1}{5\cdot5\cdot9\cdot9}$, to equal $\frac{1}{2025}$.

7. When you multiply any whole number, fraction, or decimal by 0, your answer is 0.

8. Expand $\left(\frac{3}{8}\right)^3(2)$ to equal $\frac{3}{8}\times\frac{3}{8}\times\frac{3}{8}\times 2$. Cancel the 2 in the numerator with one of the 8s in the denominator, $\frac{3}{8}\times\frac{3}{8}\times\frac{3}{\cancel{8}_4}\times\cancel{2}^1$. Multiply your remaining numerators and denominators, $\frac{3\times3\times3}{8\times8\times4}$, to equal $\frac{27}{256}$.

9. Expand $\left(\frac{2}{3}\right)^3\left(\frac{1}{2}\right)^4\left(\frac{6}{11}\right)$ to $\left(\frac{2}{3}\right)\left(\frac{2}{3}\right)\left(\frac{2}{3}\right)\left(\frac{1}{2}\right)\left(\frac{1}{2}\right)\left(\frac{1}{2}\right)\left(\frac{1}{2}\right)\left(\frac{6}{11}\right)$. Cancel the three 2s in the numerator with three of the 2s in the denominator. Also, since 3 is a common factor to both 6 and 3, use canceling to divide 3 into both 6 and 3. Cancel the two remaining 2s. Notice that 6 is canceled to 2, then 2 is canceled to 1. $\frac{\cancel{2}^1}{3}\cdot\frac{\cancel{2}^1}{3}\cdot\frac{\cancel{2}^1}{\cancel{3}_1}\cdot\frac{1}{\cancel{2}_1}\cdot\frac{1}{\cancel{2}_1}\cdot\frac{1}{\cancel{2}_1}\cdot\frac{1}{\cancel{2}_1}\cdot\frac{\cancel{6}\,\cancel{2}^1}{11}$. Now, multiply your remaining numerators and denominators, $\frac{1}{3\cdot3\cdot11}$ to equal $\frac{1}{99}$.

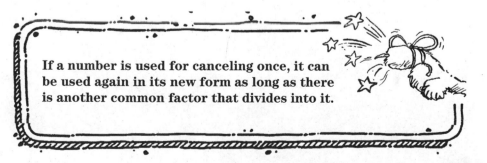

If a number is used for canceling once, it can be used again in its new form as long as there is another common factor that divides into it.

10. Since 10 is a whole number, $10^2 = 10 \cdot 10 = 100$, and $\left(\frac{2}{5}\right)^2 = \frac{2}{5} \times \frac{2}{5} = \frac{4}{25}$. Now multiply $100 \cdot \frac{4}{25}$. Cancel the 25 and the 100, since 25 is a common factor to both 25 and 100, $\overset{4}{100} \cdot \frac{4}{\underset{1}{25}}$. Multiply $4 \cdot 4$ to get the answer of 16.

CHAPTER EIGHT

Outrageous Order of Operations

If your numbers are in great disorder,
Using PEMDAS will put them in order.

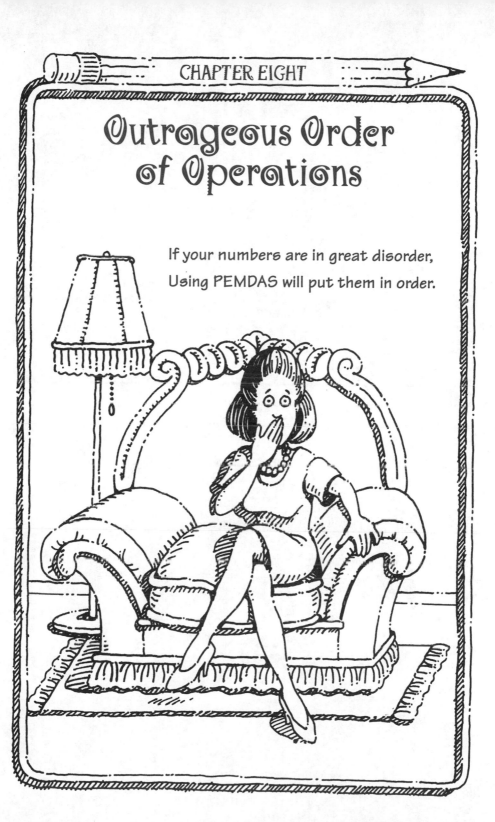

STRATEGY AND SAMPLES

Okay, here's the order of operations

I'll have 2 additions and 1 multiplication to go, please.

No, No, the order of operations in mathematics refers to a prescribed way of doing a math problem. The order can be described as follows:

1. Perform all operations inside **p**arentheses or with **e**xponents as they occur from *left to right* in the problem.

2. Perform any **m**ultiplications or **d**ivisions as they occur from *left to right* in the problem.

3. Perform any **a**dditions or **s**ubtractions as they occur from *left to right* in the problem.

This order of operations can easily be remembered by the letters **PEMDAS** and the phrase "**P**lease **e**xcuse **m**y **d**ear **A**unt **S**ally."

Level 1	Level 2	Level 3
P E	M D	A S

These three levels form a hierarchy, as in a castle. For example, in a castle the highest level is the King or Queen, the middle level is the Prince or Princess, and the lowest level is non-royalty. First we must tend to the King and Queen. Next we take care of the Prince and Princess. Finally, we attend to the male and female non-royalty.

Both operations on each level are equal in importance to each other. Therefore, "as they occur from left to right" means that if division occurs before multiplication in a problem, you do the division first. (Who gets dinner first, the King or Queen? The rule is that whoever you *see* first gets his or her dinner first.) Likewise, do the same for each of the other levels.

For example, find $3 + 2 \times 4$.

1. In the order of operations, multiplication is performed before addition, so multiply the 2 times 4 first.

2. The problem now looks like $3 + 8$.

3. Perform the addition to find the answer of 11.

When fractions are involved, the same rules apply.

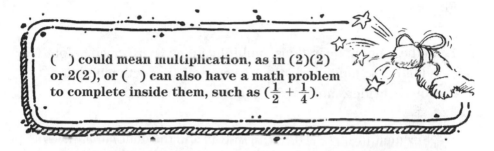

( ) could mean multiplication, as in (2)(2) or 2(2), or ( ) can also have a math problem to complete inside them, such as $(\frac{1}{2} + \frac{1}{4})$.

Orderly Combo #1

Find $\left(\frac{1}{2} + \frac{1}{3}\right) \times 2$.

1. Perform the operations inside the parentheses first. Therefore, add $\frac{1}{2} + \frac{1}{3}$ using the fraction rules. To do this, use the common denominator of 6 and convert each fraction to sixths. So, $\frac{1}{2} = \frac{3}{6}$ because $6 \div 2 = 3$ and $1 \cdot 3 = 3$, and $\frac{1}{3} = \frac{2}{6}$ because $6 \div 3 = 2$ and $1 \cdot 2 = 2$.

2. The problem now looks like $\frac{3}{6} + \frac{2}{6}$.

3. Add the numerators (in this case $3 + 2 = 5$).

4. The answer is $\frac{5}{6}$.

5. Replace the $\frac{1}{2} + \frac{1}{3}$ with $\frac{5}{6}$ in the original problem.

6. The problem now looks like $\frac{5}{6} \times 2$.

7. Use cancellation with multiplication to divide 2 into 6 and 2 into 2, $\frac{5}{{}_3\cancel{6}} \times \cancel{2}^1$

8. The problem now looks like $\frac{5}{3} \times 1$.

9. Multiply. The answer is $\frac{5}{3}$ or $1\frac{2}{3}$.

Orderly Combo #2

Find $\frac{1}{4} + \frac{3}{5} \times \frac{2}{8}$.

1. In the order of operations, multiplication is performed before addition, so multiply $\frac{3}{5} \times \frac{2}{8}$. Use cancellation with multiplication to divide 2 into 8 and 2 into 2, $\frac{3}{5} \times \frac{\cancel{2}^1}{{}_4\cancel{8}}$ to get $\frac{3}{5} \times \frac{1}{4}$.

2. Now multiply across the numerators and the denominators to get $\frac{3}{20}$.

3. The problem now looks like $\frac{1}{4} + \frac{3}{20}$. Use the common denominator of 20 and change $\frac{1}{4}$ into twentieths. So, $\frac{1}{4} = \frac{5}{20}$ because 20 divided by 4 equals 5 and 1 multiplied by 5 equals 5.

4. The problem now looks like $\frac{5}{20} + \frac{3}{20}$.

5. Since the denominators are the same, just add the numerators and keep the denominator, $\frac{5}{20} + \frac{3}{20} = \frac{8}{20}$.

6. Since 4 divides evenly into both 8 and 20, you can reduce your fraction to the simplest form by dividing 4 into 8 and 20, $\frac{\cancel{8}^2}{{}_5\cancel{20}}$, to get $\frac{2}{5}$.

7. The answer is $\frac{2}{5}$.

Orderly Combo #3

Find $7\frac{7}{8} - \left(\frac{5}{6} \div \frac{1}{3}\right)^2$.

1. By the order of operations, parentheses and exponents are on the same level (like the King and Queen), so since the parentheses occur first from left to right, perform the operations in the parentheses first.

2. Divide $\frac{5}{6}$ by $\frac{1}{3}$ by changing $\frac{1}{3}$ to its reciprocal and multiplying.

3. The part inside the parentheses looks like $\left(\frac{5}{6} \times \frac{3}{1}\right)$.

4. Use canceling to divide the 3 and the 6 by 3, $\frac{5}{{}_2\cancel{6}} \times \frac{\cancel{3}^1}{1}$.

5. You now have $\left(\frac{5}{2} \times \frac{1}{1}\right) = \frac{5}{2}$.

6. Square the $\frac{5}{2}$ to equal $\frac{25}{4}$.
$$\left(\frac{5}{2}\right)^2 = \frac{5}{2} \times \frac{5}{2} = \frac{25}{4}$$

7. Change the $\frac{25}{4}$ to the mixed number $6\frac{1}{4}$ by dividing 4 into 25.

8. Now substitute $6\frac{1}{4}$ back in the original problem in place of the parentheses and exponent.

9. The problem now looks like $7\frac{7}{8} - 6\frac{1}{4}$.

10. Use a common denominator of 8. Rewrite the $6\frac{1}{4}$ with a denominator of eighths, $6\frac{1}{4} = 6\frac{2}{8}$ because $8 \div 4 = 2$ and $1 \times 2 = 2$.

11. Perform the subtraction $7\frac{7}{8} - 6\frac{2}{8}$.

12. Keep the denominators and subtract the numerators, $\frac{7}{8} - \frac{2}{8} = \frac{5}{8}$.

13. Subtract the whole numbers ($7 - 6 = 1$). The answer is $1\frac{5}{8}$.

BRAIN TICKLERS
Set # 11

Use the order of operations to simplify these funtastic fractions:

1. $\left(3\frac{1}{2} - 2\right) \div 3 + 1\frac{3}{4}$

2. $\left(\frac{5}{12} + \frac{1}{3}\right)^2$

3. $\left(\frac{3}{5}\right)^3 - \frac{3}{25}$

4. $16 - \left(\frac{1}{4} \cdot \frac{8}{11}\right) + \left(\frac{1}{2}\right)^2$

5. $\left(2\frac{1}{4} - \frac{1}{8}\right) \div \left(\frac{5}{8} + \frac{1}{4}\right)$

6. $\frac{1}{2} + 3\frac{1}{3} \times 6 \div \left(\frac{1}{3}\right)^2 - 1$

7. $\frac{1}{2} + \frac{3}{4} \div \frac{1}{3}$

8. $1\frac{1}{3} + \frac{6}{7} \times \frac{14}{15}$

9. $\frac{3}{4}\left(\frac{4}{9}\right)^2 + \frac{1}{2}$

10. $\left(\frac{3}{4}\right)^2 \div \left(\frac{3}{8} - \frac{1}{12}\right)$

(Answers are on pages 127–132.)

BRAIN TICKLERS—THE ANSWERS

Set # 11, page 126

Follow PEMDAS for all problems below.

1. Perform subtraction *inside the parentheses* first. In $3\frac{1}{2} - 2$, subtract the whole numbers and bring along the fraction to your answer. So $3\frac{1}{2} - 2 = 1\frac{1}{2}$. The problem now looks like $1\frac{1}{2} \div 3 + 1\frac{3}{4}$. Using PEMDAS, *division* is the next operation to perform. This section of your problem is $1\frac{1}{2} \div 3$. Change $1\frac{1}{2}$ to the improper fraction of $\frac{3}{2}$. Now you have $\frac{3}{2} \div 3$. Change 3 to its reciprocal of $\frac{1}{3}$ and multiply, $\frac{3}{2} \cdot \frac{1}{3}$. Cancel the two 3s, $\frac{1\cancel{3}}{2} \cdot \frac{1}{\cancel{3}_1}$. This part of your answer equals $\frac{1}{2}$. The original problem is now simplified to $\frac{1}{2} + 1\frac{3}{4}$. Now, your last operation to perform is *addition*. Find a common denominator for 2 and 4. The LCM is 4. Rewrite $\frac{1}{2}$ with the common denominator of 4, $\frac{1}{2} = \frac{?}{4}$. Divide 2 into 4 and multiply the result by 1, $4 \div 2 = 2$ and $2 \cdot 1 = 2$. So, $\frac{1}{2} = \frac{2}{4}$. Now your problem looks like $\frac{2}{4} + 1\frac{3}{4}$. Add the two fractions and bring along the whole number, $\frac{2}{4} + 1\frac{3}{4} = 1\frac{5}{4}$. Change $\frac{5}{4}$ to the mixed number $1\frac{1}{4}$ by dividing 4 into 5 and getting a fractional remainder. You now have $1\frac{5}{4} = 1 + 1\frac{1}{4}$. Add your two whole numbers and bring along your fraction, $1 + 1\frac{1}{4} = 2\frac{1}{4}$. Your final answer is $2\frac{1}{4}$.

2. Perform the addition operation *inside the parentheses*. Find a common denominator for 12 and 3. The LCM is 12. Rewrite $\frac{1}{3}$ with the new denominator of 12, $\frac{1}{3} = \frac{?}{12}$. Divide 3 into 12 and multiply the result by 1, $12 \div 3 = 4$ and $4 \times 1 = 4$.

So, $\frac{1}{3} = \frac{4}{12}$. The fraction $\frac{5}{12}$ stays the same because it already has the common denominator of 12. Add $\frac{5}{12} + \frac{4}{12}$ to equal $\frac{9}{12}$. Reduce $\frac{9}{12}$ by dividing the common factor of 3 into both the numerator and the denominator, $\frac{9\,^3}{4\,12}$. The fraction is $\frac{3}{4}$ in simplest form. The problem now becomes $\left(\frac{3}{4}\right)^2$. To *square* $\frac{3}{4}$, multiply $\frac{3}{4} \times \frac{3}{4}$. Your answer is $\frac{9}{16}$.

3. In this problem, simplify the portion with the *exponent* first. If you multiply your numerators and denominators, you get $\frac{27}{125}$. Your original problem now looks like $\frac{27}{125} - \frac{3}{25}$. Now do the *subtraction* by finding a common denominator for 25 and 125. The LCM is 125. Rewrite $\frac{3}{25}$ with the new denominator of 125, $\frac{3}{25} = \frac{?}{125}$, by dividing 25 into 125 and multiplying the result by 3. So, $\frac{3}{25} = \frac{15}{125}$. The fraction $\frac{27}{125}$ stays the same because it already has the common denominator. Set up your subtraction to look like $\frac{27}{125} - \frac{15}{125}$. Subtract the two numerators to get $\frac{12}{125}$.

4. The first operation to perform here is the multiplication within the *parentheses*, $\left(\frac{1}{4} \cdot \frac{8}{11}\right)$. Since 4 is a common factor to both 4 and 8, you can use canceling to simplify, $\left(\frac{1}{{}_1 4} \cdot \frac{8\,^2}{11}\right)$. Multiply what's left to get a result of $\frac{2}{11}$ in parentheses. The problem now looks like $16 - \frac{2}{11} + \left(\frac{1}{2}\right)^2$. The second operation to perform here involves the *exponent*, $\left(\frac{1}{2}\right)^2$. Multiply $\frac{1}{2} \cdot \frac{1}{2}$ to equal $\frac{1}{4}$. You now have $16 - \frac{2}{11} + \frac{1}{4}$. Now because addition and subtraction are on equal levels of importance, do what comes first in the problem from left to right. So, *subtraction* is next, $16 - \frac{2}{11}$. Change the 16 into $15\frac{11}{11}$ by subtracting 1 whole from the 16, making it a 15, and trading the 1 whole for $\frac{11}{11}$. Now subtract $15\frac{11}{11} - \frac{2}{11}$ by subtracting

the two fractions and bringing along the whole number. The result of the subtraction is $15\frac{9}{11}$. The problem now looks like $15\frac{9}{11} + \frac{1}{4}$. Now, *addition* is the only operation left. Find a common denominator for 4 and 11. The LCM of 4 and 11 is 44. Rewrite $\frac{9}{11}$ as $\frac{?}{44}$ by dividing 11 into 44 and multiplying the result by 9, $44 \div 11 = 4$ and $4 \cdot 9 = 36$. So, $\frac{9}{11} = \frac{36}{44}$. Similarly $\frac{1}{4} = \frac{11}{44}$. The problem now looks like $15\frac{36}{44} + \frac{11}{44}$. Add the two numerators and bring along the whole number to get $15\frac{47}{44}$. Rewrite $\frac{47}{44}$ as the mixed number $1\frac{3}{44}$. You now have $15 + 1\frac{3}{44}$. Add to get $16\frac{3}{44}$.

5. First, work with subtraction inside the first *parentheses* from left to right, $(2\frac{1}{4} - \frac{1}{8})$. Find a common denominator for 4 and 8. The LCM is 8. Rewrite $2\frac{1}{4}$ as $2\frac{?}{8}$ by dividing 4 into 8 and multiplying the result by 1, $8 \div 4 = 2$ and $2 \cdot 1 = 2$. So, $2\frac{1}{4} = 2\frac{2}{8}$. Keep $\frac{1}{8}$ the same because it already has the common denominator of 8. Subtract $2\frac{2}{8} - \frac{1}{8}$ to equal $2\frac{1}{8}$. Now, work with addition inside the second *parentheses*. To add $\frac{5}{8} + \frac{1}{4}$ you need a common denominator of 8 as found above. Change $\frac{1}{4}$ into $\frac{2}{8}$ by the same procedure as above and add this to the $\frac{5}{8}$, $\frac{5}{8} + \frac{2}{8} = \frac{7}{8}$. The original problem is now changed to $2\frac{1}{8} \div \frac{7}{8}$. Your last operation is *division*. Rewrite $2\frac{1}{8}$ as the improper fraction $\frac{17}{8}$. Then change $\frac{7}{8}$ to its reciprocal of $\frac{8}{7}$ and multiply, $\frac{17}{8} \cdot \frac{8}{7}$. Now, the two 8s will cancel, $\frac{17}{8^1} \cdot \frac{8^1}{7}$. Multiply your remaining numbers to get $\frac{17}{7}$. Change this improper fraction to a mixed number by dividing 7 into 17 with a fractional remainder. Your final simplified answer is $2\frac{3}{7}$.

6. According to PEMDAS, the *exponent* should be worked on first in this problem. Here, $\left(\frac{1}{3}\right)^2 = \frac{1}{3} \cdot \frac{1}{3}$. Multiply the numerators and denominators to equal $\frac{1}{9}$. The next operation in order is multiplication. Multiply $3\frac{1}{3} \times 6$. Rewrite $3\frac{1}{3}$ as the improper fraction $\frac{10}{3}$. You now have $\frac{10}{3} \cdot 6$. Since 3 is a common factor to both 3 and 6, you can use canceling to show the division, $\frac{10}{1\cancel{3}} \cdot \cancel{6}^2$. Multiply the remaining numbers to get 20. The original problem now is changed to $\frac{1}{2} + 20 \div \frac{1}{9} - 1$. The third operation here is *division*. The division part is $20 \div \frac{1}{9}$. Change $\frac{1}{9}$ to its reciprocal of 9 and change the problem to multiplication, $20 \cdot \frac{9}{1}$. Multiply to get 180. The original problem now looks like $\frac{1}{2} + 180 - 1$. Since addition and subtraction are on the same level, perform *addition* first because it occurs first from left to right. So, $\frac{1}{2} + 180 = 180\frac{1}{2}$, and then $180\frac{1}{2} - 1 = 179\frac{1}{2}$ by performing the final operation of *subtraction*.

7. Here division is the first operation to perform. With $\frac{3}{4} \div \frac{1}{3}$, invert the $\frac{1}{3}$ to its reciprocal of $\frac{3}{1}$ and change the problem to multiplication, $\frac{3}{4} \times \frac{3}{1}$. Multiply to get $\frac{9}{4}$. Now you have the addition problem $\frac{1}{2} + \frac{9}{4}$. Since 4 is the common denominator, rewrite $\frac{1}{2}$ with the new denominator of 4, $\frac{1}{2} = \frac{?}{4}$, by dividing 2 into 4 and multiplying the result by 1 to get $\frac{1}{2} = \frac{2}{4}$. Now add $\frac{2}{4} + \frac{9}{4}$. Your answer is $\frac{11}{4}$ by adding the two numerators. Rewrite $\frac{11}{4}$ as the mixed number $2\frac{3}{4}$. Your final answer is $2\frac{3}{4}$.

8. *Multiplication* is the first operation to perform here according to PEMDAS. In the section $\frac{6}{7} \times \frac{14}{15}$, you can divide 7 into both 7 and 14, since 7 is a common factor of both 7 and 14, $\frac{6}{1^7} \cdot \frac{14^2}{15}$. Since 3 is a common factor of both 6 and 15, divide 3 into both 6 and 15, $\frac{^2 6}{1} \cdot \frac{2}{15_5}$. Multiply your numerators and denominators to get $\frac{4}{5}$. Now your problem looks like $1\frac{1}{3} + \frac{4}{5}$. *Add* by finding a common denominator for 5 and 3. The LCM is 15. Rewrite $\frac{4}{5}$ with the common denominator of 15, $\frac{4}{5} = \frac{?}{15}$. Divide 5 into 15 and multiply the result by 4, 15 ÷ 5 = 3 and 3 · 4 = 12. Now, $\frac{4}{5} = \frac{12}{15}$. Similarly, $1\frac{1}{3} = 1\frac{5}{15}$. Now add $1\frac{5}{15} + \frac{12}{15}$. Bring along the whole number and add the two fractions, $1\frac{5}{15} + \frac{12}{15} = 1\frac{17}{15}$. Rewrite $\frac{17}{15}$ as the mixed number $1\frac{2}{15}$. Now you have $1 + 1\frac{2}{15}$. Add the two whole numbers and bring along the fraction, $1 + 1\frac{2}{15} = 2\frac{2}{15}$. The simplified answer is $2\frac{2}{15}$.

9. The portion with the exponent $\left(\frac{4}{9}\right)^2$, can be simplified to $\frac{16}{81}$ by multiplying 4 · 4 for the numerator and 9 · 9 for the denominator. The problem now reads $\frac{3}{4} \cdot \frac{16}{81} + \frac{1}{2}$. Perform *multiplication* next, $\frac{3}{4} \cdot \frac{16}{81}$. Cancel the 3 from the numerator with the 81 in the denominator and, similarly, the 4 in the denominator with the 16 in the numerator, $\frac{1\cancel{3}}{1\cancel{4}} \cdot \frac{\cancel{16}^4}{\cancel{81}_{27}}$. The result is $\frac{4}{27}$. Now the problem looks like $\frac{4}{27} + \frac{1}{2}$. To perform the last operation of *addition*, find a common denominator for 27 and 2. The LCM is 54. Rewrite $\frac{4}{27}$ with the common denominator of 54 by dividing 27 into 54 and multiplying the result by 4, $\frac{4}{27} = \frac{8}{54}$. Similarly, $\frac{1}{2} = \frac{27}{54}$. Now add $\frac{8}{54} + \frac{27}{54}$. Add the two numerators to equal $\frac{35}{54}$.

10. Here, the operation with the *exponent*, $\left(\frac{3}{4}\right)^2$, is the first operation to perform, $\left(\frac{3}{4}\right)^2 = \frac{3 \cdot 3}{4 \cdot 4} = \frac{9}{16}$. Now you have $\frac{9}{16} \div \left(\frac{3}{8} - \frac{1}{12}\right)$. Next work with the operation inside the *parentheses*. This is the subtraction problem $\frac{3}{8} - \frac{1}{12}$. Find a common denominator for 8 and 12. The LCM is 24. Rewrite $\frac{3}{8}$ into the new denominator of 24 by dividing 8 into 24 and multiplying this number by 3, $\frac{3}{8} = \frac{9}{24}$. Similarly, $\frac{1}{12} = \frac{2}{24}$. Subtract $\frac{9}{24} - \frac{2}{24}$. This part of the answer is $\frac{7}{24}$. Your original problem now looks like $\frac{9}{16} \div \frac{7}{24}$. The third and last operation to perform in this problem is *division*. Invert $\frac{7}{24}$ to its reciprocal of $\frac{24}{7}$. Set up the multiplication problem $\frac{9}{16} \cdot \frac{24}{7}$. The greatest common factor (GCF) of 16 and 24 is 8. Use canceling to divide 8 into both numbers, $\frac{9}{{}_2\cancel{16}} \cdot \frac{\cancel{24}^3}{7}$. Multiply the remaining numbers to get $\frac{27}{14}$. Rewrite $\frac{27}{14}$ as a mixed number by dividing 14 into 27. Your final answer is $1\frac{13}{14}$.

CHAPTER NINE

Refreshing Ratios, Remarkable Rates, and Popular Proportions

1 to 2, 3 to 4

Rates and proportions

Are fun to explore.

REFRESHING RATIOS

A **ratio** of two numbers is a comparison of the numbers using the same units. A ratio can be expressed as a fraction, with a colon, or with the word "to." Ratios should be expressed in simplest form, where the numbers in the numerator and denominator have no common factors.

AWESOME:

A ratio of 1 to 2 = 1 : 2 = $\frac{1}{2}$

AWFUL:

A ratio of 6 to 3 = 6 : 3 = $\frac{6}{3}$ (not in simplest form; $\frac{2}{1}$ would be better)

Exquisite Example

Express as a ratio: \$3 to \$5. Since dollars is the same unit for both parts, the label of the units can be eliminated in your answer. The answer can be expressed as 3 to 5, 3 : 5, or $\frac{3}{5}$.

Another Exquisite Example

What is the ratio of 4 coins to 12 coins? The answer can be expressed as 4 to 12, 4 : 12, or $\frac{4}{12}$. Since the numbers 4 and 12 both have common factors of 2 and 4, you can use either to simplify your fraction.

If you use the GCF, you will have fewer steps than if you use another factor. Since 4 is the GCF, divide 4 into both 4 and 12 to simplify your ratio to 1 to 3, or 1 : 3, or $\frac{1}{3}$.

Still Another Exquisite Example

What is the ratio of 6 cups to 2 cups? The answer can be expressed as 6 to 2, 6 : 2, or $\frac{6}{2}$. Since 6 and 2 have a common GCF of 2, you can divide 2 into both 6 and 2 to simplify your ratio to 3 to 1, 3 : 1, or $\frac{3}{1}$.

And Yet Another Exquisite Example

What is the ratio of 8 hours to 1 day? Change "1 day" into 24 hours so that the ratio can be compared in the same units. The answer can then be expressed as 8 to 24, 8 : 24, or $\frac{8}{24}$. Since 8 and 24 have a greatest common factor of 8, simplify your ratio to 1 to 3, 1 : 3, or $\frac{1}{3}$.

• •

NOTE: Hereafter in this book we will express ratios in the fraction form only.

Ratios can also be used in word problems. The word or words that come before the word "to" form the numerator of your ratio, and the word or words after the word "to" form the denominator of the ratio.

Beautiful Example

Tae rode his bike 10 miles on Saturday and 12 miles on Sunday. What is the ratio of his miles on Saturday to his miles on Sunday?

Set up a ratio: $\dfrac{\text{miles on Saturday}}{\text{miles on Sunday}}$

The miles on Saturday are 10 and the miles on Sunday are 12, so your fractional ratio becomes $\frac{10}{12}$. Since 2 is a common factor to both 10 and 12, you can use canceling $\frac{\cancel{10}^{5}}{\cancel{12}_{6}}$, to simplify your fraction to $\frac{5}{6}$. Therefore, the ratio of Tae's miles on Saturday to Tae's miles on Sunday is $\frac{5}{6}$.

Satisfying Example

Loribeth's winning softball team scored 14 runs in the champion-ship game. The losing team scored 8 runs.

a) What is the ratio of the winning score to the losing score?

Set up a ratio: $\dfrac{\text{winning score}}{\text{losing score}}$

The winning score is equal to 14 runs and the losing score is equal to 8 runs, so your fractional ratio becomes $\frac{14}{8}$. Since 2 is a common factor to both 14 and 8, you can use canceling, $\dfrac{\overset{7}{\cancel{14}}}{\underset{4}{\cancel{8}}}$, to simplify your fraction to $\frac{7}{4}$. Therefore, the ratio of the winning score to the losing score is $\frac{7}{4}$.

b) What is the ratio of the number of winning runs scored *to* the *total* number of runs scored?

Set up a ratio: $\dfrac{\text{winning runs scored}}{\text{total runs scored}}$

The winning runs scored are equal to 14 and the total runs scored can be obtained by adding winning runs plus losing runs. Since the number of winning runs is 14 and the number of losing runs is 8, the total number of runs is equal to $14 + 8 = 22$. The fractional ratio is $\frac{14}{22}$. Since 2 is a common factor to both 14 and 22, you can use canceling, $\frac{\cancel{14}^{7}}{\cancel{22}_{11}}$, to simplify your fraction to $\frac{7}{11}$. Therefore, the ratio of the winning score to the total score is $\frac{7}{11}$.

• •

Pleasurable Example

600 people attended the school play on Friday night. 350 people attended on Saturday night. What is the ratio of attendance on Friday *to* the attendance on Saturday?

Set up a ratio: $\dfrac{\text{Friday's attendance}}{\text{Saturday's attendance}}$

Friday's attendance is equal to 600 and Saturday's attendance is equal to 350, so the fractional ratio is $\frac{600}{350}$. Since 50 is a common factor to both 600 and 350, you can use canceling, $\frac{\cancel{600}^{12}}{\cancel{350}_{7}}$, to reduce your fraction to $\frac{12}{7}$. Therefore, the ratio of Friday's attendance to Saturday's attendance is $\frac{12}{7}$.

• •

BRAIN TICKLERS
Set # 12

Write each comparison as a ratio in simplest form using a fraction:

1. $640 to $820

2. 8 days to 20 days

3. 75 cents to 50 cents

4. 10 feet to 10 feet

5. 30 minutes to 1 hour

Set up and solve each word problem as a ratio in simplest form:

6. Mr. Foschi bought a high-definition flat screen television in an appliance store for $560. Mr. Green bought his high-definition flat screen television in a department store for $620. Find the ratio of the price of the appliance store television *to* the price of the department store television.

7. Micky can type 40 words per minute, while his sister can type only 28 words per minute. What is the ratio of Micky's typing speed *to* his sister's typing speed?

8. The home economics class used 5 cups of sugar, 3 cups of flour, and 2 cups of water to stir into its cupcake batter.

    a) What is the ratio of sugar *to* water?
    b) What is the ratio of flour *to* the total ingredients listed above?

9. The price of a candy bar increased from $.65 to $1.05 in a year. What is the ratio of the increase in price *to* the original price?

10. Steve's dad bought a computer 3 years ago for $2000. Today the computer is worth $800 due to depreciation. Find the ratio of the computer's depreciation (decrease in value) *to* its original cost.

(Answers are on pages 155–157.)

REMARKABLE RATES

A **rate** is a comparison of two quantities using *different* units. It is written as a fraction.

RIGHT:

8 pounds of meat per 5 people $= \frac{8}{5}$

12 pounds of grass seed per 5 trees $= \frac{12}{5}$

WRONG:

$\frac{8 \text{ girls}}{7 \text{ girls}}$ (This is a *ratio* because it has the *same* units.)

Rates should be expressed in simplest form, where the numbers in the numerator and denominator have no common factors.

A special kind of rate, known as a **unit rate**, is one in which the denominator is 1.

CORRECT:

15 miles per hour $= \dfrac{15 \text{ miles}}{1 \text{ hour}}$

CRUMMY:

$\dfrac{15 \text{ miles}}{4 \text{ hours}}$

To find a unit rate, divide your denominator into your numerator.

GREAT:

$15.60 for 3 hours = 15.60 ÷ 3 = $3\overline{)15.60}^{\,5.20}$ = $5.20 for 1 hour.

$$\frac{\$15.60}{3 \text{ hours}} = \frac{\$5.20}{1 \text{ hour}}$$

GRAND:

6 cupcakes for 3 people = 6 ÷ 3 = $3\overline{)6}^{\,2}$ = 2 cupcakes for 1 person.

$$\frac{6 \text{ cupcakes}}{3 \text{ people}} = \frac{2 \text{ cupcakes}}{1 \text{ person}}$$

GRACEFUL:

78 gallons of gas for 4 miles = 78 ÷ 4 = $4\overline{)78.0}^{\,19.5}$ = 19.5 gallons of gas for 1 mile.

$$\frac{78 \text{ gallons of gas}}{4 \text{ miles}} = \frac{19.5 \text{ gallons of gas}}{1 \text{ mile}}$$

Rates can also be used in word problems. The words and numbers that come before prepositional words such as "**to**," "**for**," "**on**," and "**in**" form the numerator of your rate written as a fraction, and the word or words after these prepositional words form the denominator of your rate written as a fraction. Unit rate word problems often contain words "**per**" or "**each**."

There are two ways to put your rate in simplest form.

1. Divide the GCF into both the numerator and denominator. Simplify the fraction.
2. Divide the denominator into the numerator to get a unit rate, a rate with 1 unit in the denominator.

In many problems the rate in simplest form is the unit rate.

Here are some examples of writing rates in simplest form:

DANDY:

2400 words on 120 pages

Set up a rate: $\dfrac{2400 \text{ words}}{120 \text{ pages}}$

Divide 120 into 2400. $\quad 120\overline{)2400}^{20}$.

The new rate is $\dfrac{20 \text{ words}}{1 \text{ page}}$

The rate of 20 words on 1 page is the unit rate, which is in simplest form.

DELIGHTFUL:

28 children in 8 cars

Set up a rate: $\dfrac{28 \text{ children}}{8 \text{ cars}}$

The GCF between 28 and 8 is 4, so divide 4 into both the numerator and denominator.

$$\frac{28 \text{ children}}{8 \text{ cars}} = \frac{7 \text{ children}}{2 \text{ cars}}$$

The rate in simplest form is 7 children in 2 cars. Also, if you divide 2 into 7,

$$\begin{array}{r} 3 \\ 2\overline{)7} \\ \underline{6} \\ 1 \end{array}$$

you get an answer of $3\frac{1}{2}$. So, $3\frac{1}{2}$ children in 1 car is your *unit* rate. Both ways to express your rate in simplest form are correct, but because $\frac{1}{2}$ child doesn't make sense, it is better to leave your rate as 7 children in 2 cars in this problem.

WORTHY:

Jené works at a gas station after school and on weekends. She worked 24 hours last week and earned $146.40 for the week. How much did she make *per* hour?

The word "per" refers to a rate with 1 unit in the denominator, or a unit rate. Divide the number of hours into the total salary for the week to find the salary per hour,

$$\begin{array}{r} 6.10 \\ 24\overline{)146.40} \end{array}$$

Jené's salary per hour is $6.10.

JOLLY:

The total cost of making 1150 pairs of jeans in the factory is $10,450. If 150 pairs are discarded due to irregularities, what is the cost *per* pair of jeans for those that are not discarded?

The word "per" refers to a unit rate. First subtract the number of discards from the total number of jeans, $1150 - 150 = 1000$. Now, divide the number of jeans that are not discarded into the total price of making all the jeans, $10,450 \div 1000 = 10.45$. The cost per pair of jeans that are not discarded is $10.45.

It is often helpful to determine a "better" or "best " buy when making purchases. To do this, simply compare the unit prices between your quantities and see which is less. This can also be extended to comparisons of unit rates other than prices.

Superbuy Market is selling a string of 12 hot dogs for $7.08. Green's Market is selling the same hot dogs at 10 for $5.95. Which store has the better buy?

To find the unit price for 1 hot dog at each store:

Superbuy

Set up your rate, $\frac{\$7.08}{12}$, and divide the denominator into the numerator to get a unit rate of $.59 per hot dog.

Green's

Set up your rate, $\frac{\$5.95}{10}$, and divide the denominator into the numerator to get a unit rate of $.595 per hot dog.

The unit prices are very close but $.59 is a little lower than $.595, so the store with the better price would be Superbuy Market.

BRAIN TICKLERS
Set # 13

Write as a rate or unit rate in simplest form:

1. $56 for 4 shirts

2. 75 cents for 5 pieces of gum

3. 168 miles in 4 hours

4. 30 books on 8 shelves

5. 250 trees planted on 5 acres

Set up and solve each word problem as a rate in simplest form:

6. The Cityview Movie Theater charges $19.80 for 4 adult matinee movie tickets. How much does each ticket cost?

7. A toy company sold 550 mini-footballs for $4174.50. What is the price per football?

8. A new plane travels 2100 miles in $2\frac{1}{2}$ hours. Find the plane's speed in miles per hour.

9. The total cost of producing 2000 baseball cards was $220.80. Of these cards, 160 had to be discarded due to imperfections. What is the cost per card of those baseball cards that were not discarded?

10. The students in Mrs. Jamison's English class want to read 77 books in $3\frac{1}{2}$ weeks. How many books per week should they read?

11. Dark chocolate-covered pretzels cost $5.98 for 16 pretzels. White chocolate-covered pretzels cost $4.75 for 13 pretzels. Which is the better buy?

12. E-Z detergent costs $6.59 for a 64 ounce bottle. Stay Clean detergent costs $5.59 for a 50 ounce bottle. Which is the better buy?

(Answers are on pages 157–161.)

POPULAR PROPORTIONS

Two ratios or rates that are equivalent are called a **proportion**.

TRUE:

$\frac{1}{2} = \frac{2}{4}$

The cross products of a proportion are equal, $\frac{1}{2} = \frac{2}{4}$,
$1 \cdot 4 = 2 \cdot 2$.

CORRECT:

$$\frac{8 \text{ pounds}}{10 \text{ pounds}} = \frac{4 \text{ pounds}}{5 \text{ pounds}}$$

EQUIVALENT:

$$\frac{6 \text{ girls}}{7 \text{ boys}} = \frac{12 \text{ girls}}{14 \text{ boys}}$$

FALSE:

$\frac{1}{8} = \frac{1}{2}$ because $1 \cdot 8$ does not equal $1 \cdot 2$.

• •

Sometimes one of the numbers in a proportion is missing. We name this missing piece by a letter called a **variable**. You can solve the proportion for the missing piece or variable by following these steps:

1. Multiply the two cross products.

2. Set them equal to each other.

3. Divide the number on the same side as the variable into the number on the other side of the equation.

4. The result of step 3 is the missing piece to your proportion.

5. Check the cross products to make sure they are equal.

(You may want to refer to pages 23–24 for review.)

Basic Example #1

$$\frac{n}{10} = \frac{2}{5}$$
$$5 \cdot n = 10 \cdot 2$$
$$5n = 20$$

Now divide 20 by 5, $20 \div 5 = 4$.
So, $n = 4$.

Check: $4 \cdot 5 = 10 \cdot 2$
$$20 = 20$$

●●

Basic Example #2

$$\frac{15}{20} = \frac{12}{n}$$
$$15 \cdot n = 20 \cdot 12$$
$$15n = 240$$

Now divide 240 by 15, $240 \div 15 = 16$.
So, $n = 16$.

Check: $15 \cdot 16 = 240$
$$240 - 240$$

●●

The variable can be located in any one of the numerators or denominators of the proportion—the solving procedure is the same.

A Little Different Example

$$\frac{4}{n} = \frac{3}{7}$$
$$3 \cdot n = 4 \cdot 7$$
$$3n = 28$$

Now divide 28 by 3, $28 \div 3 = 9$, remainder 1.

$$\begin{array}{r} 9 \\ 3\overline{)28} \\ \underline{27} \\ 1 \end{array}$$

The remainder can be expressed as a fraction of $\frac{1}{3}$ (the remainder over the divisor).

So, $n = 9\frac{1}{3}$.

Proportions can also be used in word problems. It is often easy to set up your proportion with words first. Then replace your words with numbers in the problem. Finally, proceed to solve your proportion as described previously.

A Taxing Example

The sales tax on a $100 portable stereo purchase is $6. At this same rate, what is the tax on a $150 purchase?

1. Set up your proportion as $\frac{tax}{purchase} = \frac{tax}{purchase}$.

2. Replace your tax and purchase price as follows: $\frac{\$6}{\$100} = \frac{tax}{\$150}$
   ($6 tax and $100 purchase price go together and the unknown tax and $150 go together. We'll call the unknown tax t).

3. Multiply the cross products to get $6 \cdot 150 = 100 \cdot t$ or $900 = 100 \cdot t$.

4. Divide 100 into 900 to get an answer of $9 tax. Therefore, you can conclude that a tax of $6 on a $100 purchase is equal to a tax of $9 on a $150 purchase.

● ●

A Delicious Example

A 16-ounce box of pasta contains 210 calories. How many calories are in a 2-ounce serving of pasta?

1. Set up your proportion as $\dfrac{ounces\ of\ pasta}{calories} = \dfrac{ounces\ of\ pasta}{calories}$.

2. Replace ounces of pasta and calories from the problem as follows: $\dfrac{16}{210} = \dfrac{2}{c}$ (16 ounces and 210 calories go together, and 2 ounces of pasta and the unknown calories go together; we'll call the unknown calories c).

3. Multiply the cross products to get $16 \cdot c = 2 \cdot 210$, or $16c = 420$.

4. Divide 16 into 420,

$$
\begin{array}{r}
26 \\
16\overline{)420} \\
\underline{32} \\
100 \\
\underline{96} \\
4
\end{array}
$$

to get an answer of $26\frac{4}{16}$.

5. Reduce your fraction to get an answer of $26\frac{1}{4}$. Therefore, you can conclude that a 16-ounce box of pasta with 210 calories is equivalent to a 2-ounce serving of pasta with $26\frac{1}{4}$ calories.

● ●

BRAIN TICKLERS
Set # 14

Solve each proportion:

1. $\dfrac{6}{n} = \dfrac{4}{5}$ 2. $\dfrac{5}{8} = \dfrac{n}{10}$ 3. $\dfrac{n}{21} = \dfrac{35}{105}$

4. $\dfrac{1}{6} = \dfrac{2}{n}$ 5. $\dfrac{5}{9} = \dfrac{15}{n}$

Set up a proportion for each problem and solve:

6. Torie gets paid $165 for every 20 hours she works at the ice cream store. At this rate, what is her total salary for 16 hours?

7. The junior baseball team won 21 games out of 30 that were played. At this rate, how many games would they have won if they played 40 games?

8. Tyeesha's new television cost $299. She paid a sales tax of $17.94. At this rate, what would be the sales tax on a $350 television?

9. On a map scale, $\dfrac{3}{4}$ of an inch is equal to 120 actual miles. At the same rate, how many actual miles would a $1\frac{1}{4}$-inch scale on a map represent?

10. It takes a school bus driver 75 minutes to drive a 20-mile route. At the same rate, how many minutes would it take to drive a 12-mile route?

(Answers are on pages 161–164.)

BRAIN TICKLERS—THE ANSWERS

Set # 12, pages 141–142

1. The ratio can be expressed as $\frac{640}{820}$ in fractional form. Since both 640 and 820 end in zero, they are both divisible by 10. Dividing 10 into both the numerator and denominator produces $\frac{64}{82}$. Now, since 64 and 82 are both even numbers, use canceling to divide by 2, $\frac{\cancel{64}^{32}}{\cancel{82}_{41}}$ to get a ratio of $\frac{32}{41}$ in simplest form. If you had divided by the GCF of 20, instead of by the factor of 10, your work would have had fewer steps, but your result would be the same answer of $\frac{32}{41}$.

2. The ratio can be expressed as $\frac{8}{20}$ in fractional form. Since 4 is the GCF of 8 and 20, you can use canceling to divide 4 into both the numerator and denominator, $\frac{\cancel{8}^{2}}{\cancel{20}_{5}}$, to get a ratio of $\frac{2}{5}$ in simplest form.

3. The ratio can be expressed as $\frac{75}{50}$ in fractional form. Since 25 is the GCF of 75 and 50, use canceling to divide 25 into both your numerator and denominator, $\frac{\cancel{75}^{3}}{\cancel{50}_{2}}$, to get a ratio of $\frac{3}{2}$ in simplest form.

4. The ratio can be expressed as $\frac{10}{10}$ in fractional form. Since the numerator and denominator are the same, your ratio becomes $\frac{1}{1}$, or 1 in simplest form.

5. Since ratios must be in the same units, change 1 hour to 60 minutes. The ratio can be expressed as $\frac{30}{60}$ in fractional form. Since 30 is the GCF of 30 and 60, use canceling to divide 30 into both the numerator and denominator, $\frac{\cancel{30}^{1}}{\cancel{60}_{2}}$ to get a ratio of $\frac{1}{2}$ in simplest form.

6. The price of the appliance store television becomes the numerator (clue: these are the words *before* the word "to") and the price of the department store television becomes the denominator (clue: these are the words *after* the word "to"). The ratio looks like $\frac{560}{620}$. Use canceling to divide 20 into both 560 and 620, $\frac{\cancel{560}^{28}}{\cancel{620}_{31}}$. Your ratio in simplest form is $\frac{28}{31}$.

7. Micky's typing speed is in the numerator of the ratio and his sister's typing speed is in the denominator. The ratio looks like $\frac{40}{28}$. Since the GCF is 4, $\frac{\cancel{40}^{10}}{\cancel{28}_{7}}$, and the fraction reduces to $\frac{10}{7}$ in simplest form.

8. a) The ratio would be represented as $\frac{sugar}{water}$. The number representing sugar is 5. This number becomes the numerator. The number representing water is 2. This number becomes the denominator. Your ratio is $\frac{5}{2}$. It is in simplest form.

   b) The number representing flour becomes the numerator of 3, and the number representing total ingredients, $5 + 3 + 2 = 10$, becomes the denominator. Your ratio is $\frac{3}{10}$. It is in simplest form.

9. In this problem, $.65 is the original price of the candy bar and $1.05 is the new price. To find the increase in the price, subtract .65 from 1.05. The increase is .40. The ratio of the increase in price to the original price is $\frac{.40}{.65}$. Since 5 is the GCF of 40 and 65, divide 5 into both the numerator and the denominator and drop the decimal point representing cents, since the units are the same $\frac{\cancel{40}^{8}}{\cancel{65}_{13}}$.

   The ratio in simplest form is $\frac{8}{13}$.

10. To find the computer's depreciation, you must subtract the computer's current value from its original cost, $2000 − $800 = $1200. So, $1200 is the depreciation. Now set up a ratio with the depreciation in the numerator (clue: these are the words *before* the word "to") and the original cost in the denominator (clue: these are the words *after* the word "to"). The ratio looks like $\frac{1200}{2000}$. Now reduce the ratio to its simplest form by dividing by the GCF of 400, $\frac{\cancel{1200}^{3}}{\cancel{2000}_{5}}$. Your answer is $\frac{3}{5}$.

If you don't notice the GCF of 400, you might want to divide by 100, since both numbers end in two zeros. Then you'll have $\frac{12}{20}$. Now you can divide by 4, $\frac{\cancel{12}^{3}}{\cancel{20}_{5}}$. You'll reach the simplified form of $\frac{3}{5}$ either way.

Set # 13, pages 148–149

1. Since the word "for" separates the numerator from your denominator, set up your problem as a rate.

$$\frac{\$56}{4 \text{ shirts}}$$

You can look for a GCF for 56 and 4, which is 4, $\frac{\cancel{56}^{14}}{\cancel{4}_{1}}$. Instead of this, you can also divide 4 into 56 to get 14. The unit rate is $14 for 1 shirt.

2. Since the word "for" separates the numerator from the denominator, set up the problem as a rate.

$$\frac{75 \text{ cents}}{5 \text{ pieces of gum}}$$

You can write the rate in simplest form by dividing the GCF of 5 into both the numerator and denominator, $\frac{\overset{15}{\cancel{75}}}{\underset{1}{\cancel{5}}}$. Instead of this, you can also divide 5 into 75 to get a unit rate of 15 cents for 1 piece of gum.

3. Since the word "in" separates the numerator from the denominator, set up the problem as a rate.

$$\frac{168 \text{ miles}}{4 \text{ hours}}$$

You can simplify the rate by dividing the GCF of 4 into both your numerator and denominator, $\frac{\overset{42}{\cancel{168}}}{\underset{1}{\cancel{4}}}$. You can also get a unit rate by dividing 4 into 168. The answer is 42 miles in 1 hour in simplest form.

4. Since the word "on" separates the numerator from the denominator, set up the problem as a rate.

$$\frac{30 \text{ books}}{8 \text{ shelves}}$$

Divide the GCF of 2 into both your numerator and denominator, $\frac{\overset{15}{\cancel{30}}}{\underset{4}{\cancel{8}}}$. This produces a rate in simplest form of 15 books on 4 shelves. To get a unit rate, or the number of books on 1 shelf, divide 4 into 15 to get an answer of $3\frac{3}{4}$. The unit rate is $3\frac{3}{4}$ books on 1 shelf. Since $\frac{3}{4}$ of a book doesn't make sense, it would be better to keep the rate as 15 books on 4 shelves.

5. Since the word "on" separates the numerator from the denominator, set up the problem as a rate.

$$\frac{250 \text{ trees}}{5 \text{ acres}}$$

Since your GCF is 5, you can divide 5 into both your numerator and denominator, $\frac{\overset{50}{250}}{\underset{1}{5}}$. You can also get a unit rate by dividing 5 into 250. The rate in simplest form is 50 trees planted on 1 acre.

6. The word "each" implies a unit rate. Divide 4 into $19.80,

$$\begin{array}{r} 4.95 \\ 4\overline{)19.80} \end{array}$$

to get a price of $4.95 for each ticket.

7. The word "per" implies a unit rate. Divide 550 into $4174.50,

$$\begin{array}{r} 7.59 \\ 550\overline{)4174.50} \end{array}$$

to get a unit rate of $7.59. The price per football is $7.59.

8. Divide 2100 by $2\frac{1}{2}$ to get a unit rate. To do this, write the division with $2\frac{1}{2}$ as an improper fraction, $2100 \div \frac{5}{2}$. Invert $\frac{5}{2}$ to its reciprocal of $\frac{2}{5}$ and turn the problem into multiplication, $2100 \times \frac{2}{5}$. Since 5 divides evenly into both 5 and 2100, use canceling to simplify the problem to $420 \times \frac{2}{1}$. Multiply the numerators, 420×2, to equal 840. The plane's speed is 840 miles per hour.

9. The word "per" indicates a unit rate. First, subtract the number of imperfect cards from the total number of baseball cards, $2000 - 160 = 1840$. Now, divide the number of cards that were not discarded into the total price of producing the cards,

$$\begin{array}{r} 0.12 \\ 1840\overline{)220.80} \end{array}$$

The cost per card of the baseball cards that were not discarded is $.12.

10. The word "per" implies a unit rate. Divide 77 by $3\frac{1}{2}$ to get a unit rate. To do this, write the division with $3\frac{1}{2}$ as an improper fraction, $77 \div \frac{7}{2}$. Invert $\frac{7}{2}$ to its reciprocal of $\frac{2}{7}$ and turn the problem into multiplication, $77 \times \frac{2}{7}$. Use canceling to divide 7 into both 7 and 77, $\overset{11}{\cancel{77}} \times \frac{2}{\underset{1}{\cancel{7}}}$. The problem simplifies to $11 \times \frac{2}{1}$. Multiply the numbers remaining to get 22. The class should read 22 books per week to meet its goal.

11. To find the better buy, find the unit prices of each. Divide 16 into $5.98 to get $.37 . . . per dark chocolate pretzel and divide 13 into $4.75 to get $.36 . . . per white chocolate pretzel. Since the price per pretzel for white chocolate is cheaper than the price per pretzel for dark chocolate, the white chocolate is the better buy.

12. To determine the better buy, find the unit prices of each. Divide 64 into $6.59 to get $.10 . . . per ounce for the E-Z detergent and 50 into $5.59 to get $.11 . . . per ounce for the Stay Clean detergent. Since the E-Z detergent is cheaper per ounce, it is the better buy.

Set # 14, page 154

1. Multiply $4 \cdot n$ and set this equal to $6 \cdot 5$, $4n = 30$. Divide 4 into 30,

$$\begin{array}{r} 7 \\ 4{\overline{)30}} \\ \underline{28} \\ 2 \end{array}$$

to get an answer of $7\frac{2}{4}$. Reduce this to $7\frac{1}{2}$. Therefore, $n = 7\frac{1}{2}$.

2. Multiply $8 \cdot n$ and set this equal to $5 \cdot 10$, $8n = 50$. Divide 8 into 50,

$$\begin{array}{r} 6 \\ 8{\overline{)50}} \\ \underline{48} \\ 2 \end{array}$$

to get an answer of $6\frac{2}{8}$. Reduce this to $6\frac{1}{4}$. Therefore, $n = 6\frac{1}{4}$.

3. Multiply $105 \cdot n$ and set this equal to $21 \cdot 35$, $105n = 735$. Divide 105 into 735 to get an answer of 7. Therefore, $n = 7$.

4. Multiply $n \cdot 1$ and set this equal to $2 \cdot 6$, $1n = 12$. Therefore, $n = 12$.

5. Multiply $5 \cdot n$ and set this equal to $15 \cdot 9$, $5n = 135$. Divide 5 into 135,

$$
\begin{array}{r}
27 \\
5{\overline{)135}} \\
\underline{10} \\
35 \\
\underline{35}
\end{array}
$$

to get an answer of 27. Therefore, $n = 27$.

6. Set up your proportion as $\dfrac{salary}{number\ of\ hours} = \dfrac{salary}{number\ of\ hours}$. Replace salary and number of hours from the problem as follows: $\dfrac{165}{20} = \dfrac{s}{16}$ ($165 and 20 hours go together and 16 hours and the unknown salary go together; we'll call the unknown salary s). Multiply the cross products to get $20 \cdot s = 165 \cdot 16$, or $20s = 2640$. Divide 20 into 2640,

$$
\begin{array}{r}
132 \\
20{\overline{)2640}} \\
\underline{20} \\
64 \\
\underline{60} \\
40 \\
\underline{40}
\end{array}
$$

to get an answer of 132.

Therefore, Torie earns $132 for 16 hours.

(You can also divide $165 by 20 hours to get $8.25 per hour and then multiply $8.25 \cdot 16$ to get $132.)

7. Set up your proportion as $\frac{games\ won}{games\ played} = \frac{games\ won}{games\ played}$.
   Replace games won and games played from the problem as
   follows: $\frac{21}{30} = \frac{w}{40}$ (21 games won out of 30 games played go
   together and 40 games played and the unknown number of
   games won go together; we'll call the unknown number of
   games won w). Multiply the cross products to get $30 \cdot w =$
   $21 \cdot 40$, or $30w = 840$. Divide 30 into 840,

$$
\begin{array}{r}
28 \\
30\overline{)840} \\
\underline{60} \\
240 \\
\underline{240}
\end{array}
$$

   to get an answer of 28. Therefore, you can conclude that
   winning 21 games out of 30 is equivalent to winning 28
   games out of 40.

8. Set up your proportion as $\frac{tax}{purchase\ price} = \frac{tax}{purchase\ price}$.
   Replace the tax and purchase price from the problem as
   follows: $\frac{\$17.94}{299} = \frac{t}{350}$ (The television for $299 goes with the
   sales tax of $17.94 and the television for $350 goes with the
   unknown tax t). Multiply the cross products to get $299 \cdot t =$
   $17.94 \cdot 350$, or $299t = 6279$. Divide 299 into 6279,

$$
\begin{array}{r}
21 \\
299\overline{)6279} \\
\underline{598} \\
299 \\
\underline{299}
\end{array}
$$

   to get an answer of 21. Therefore, you can conclude that a
   sales tax of $21 on a $350 television purchase is equivalent
   to a sales tax of $17.94 on a $299 purchase.

9. Set up your proportion as $\dfrac{scale}{actual\ miles} = \dfrac{scale}{actual\ miles}$. Replace the scale and actual miles from the problem as follows:

$$\frac{\frac{3}{4}}{120} = \frac{1\frac{1}{4}}{m}$$

($\frac{3}{4}$ of an inch scale represents 120 miles and $1\frac{1}{4}$ inch represents the unknown number of miles m). Multiply the cross products to get $\frac{3}{4} \cdot m = 120 \cdot 1\frac{1}{4}$. Change $1\frac{1}{4}$ to an improper fraction to get $\frac{3}{4}m = 120 \cdot \frac{5}{4}$. Use canceling to divide 4 into both 4 and 120. Multiplying the remaining numbers gives $\frac{3}{4}m = 150$. Next, divide 150 by $\frac{3}{4}$, $150 \div \frac{3}{4}$. To do this, invert $\frac{3}{4}$ to its reciprocal of $\frac{4}{3}$ and multiply $150 \cdot \frac{4}{3}$. Use canceling to divide 3 into 150 and 3 into itself, $\overset{50}{\cancel{150}} \cdot \dfrac{4}{\underset{1}{\cancel{3}}}$. Multiply the remaining numbers to get $m = 200$. Therefore, you can conclude that a distance of $1\frac{1}{4}$ inches on the map is equal to 200 actual miles.

10. Set up your proportion as $\dfrac{minutes}{miles} = \dfrac{minutes}{miles}$. Replace the minutes and miles from the problem as follows: $\dfrac{75}{20} = \dfrac{m}{12}$ (75 minutes goes with 20 miles and the unknown number of minutes m goes with 12 miles). Multiply the cross products to get $20 \cdot m = 75 \cdot 12$, or $20m = 900$. Divide 20 into 900,

$$
\begin{array}{r}
45 \\
20\overline{)900} \\
\underline{80} \\
100 \\
\underline{100}
\end{array}
$$

to get an answer of 45. Therefore, the bus driver would drive 12 miles in 45 minutes. This is equivalent to driving 20 miles in 75 minutes.

CHAPTER TEN

The Dreaded and Disliked Word Problems

Roses are red,

Violets are blue,

If you can't figure out a whole word problem,

A fraction at a time will do.

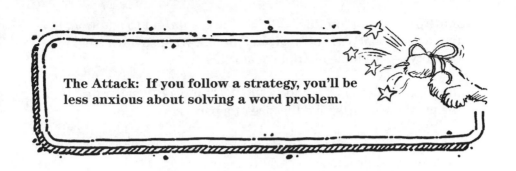

The Attack: If you follow a strategy, you'll be less anxious about solving a word problem.

STRATEGY FOR WORD PROBLEMS—PREVIEW, VIEW, DO, AND REVIEW

Preview

Skim the problem once just to get the general idea. Don't write anything down.

View

Read the problem carefully looking for important information. Look for key words or phrases, such as those below, that may appear in your problem.

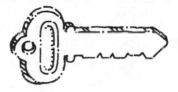

addition: "sum," "total," "altogether," "combine"

subtraction: "difference," "how much less," "how much more," "amount of decrease," "amount of increase," "how much is left"

multiplication: "product," "times," as a shortcut to addition, find a fractional part "of" a given amount, when given a single quantity—determine multiple quantities

division: "quotient," "divide," "for 1," "for each," "separate," find the number of parts, find the size of a part

If key words do not appear, some reasoning might be necessary to determine the correct operation.

Do

Plan your work. Write down the necessary steps to solve the problem. Solve it.

Review

Check your work. See if your answer makes sense and fits reasonably with the rest of the problem.

WORDY EXAMPLES

Addition

Juanita is a waitress at a diner. She works $5\frac{1}{2}$ hours on Friday, $2\frac{1}{4}$ hours on Saturday, and 6 hours on Sunday. How many hours *altogether* does she work?

1. "Altogether" is a key word for addition. Add $5\frac{1}{2}$, $2\frac{1}{4}$, and 6. Find a common denominator for 2 and 4. Use the LCM, 4, because it's the lowest number that both 2 and 4 can divide into evenly.

2. Rewrite the fractions with the common denominator: $5\frac{1}{2} = 5\frac{2}{4}$ because $4 \div 2 = 2$ and $2 \times 1 = 2$, $2\frac{1}{4} = 2\frac{1}{4}$ because 4 is already the common denominator.

3. Add the whole numbers and the fractions.

    $5 + 2 + 6 = 13$ $\qquad$ $\frac{2}{4} + \frac{1}{4} = \frac{3}{4}$

4. The answer is $13\frac{3}{4}$ hours.

Subtraction

Carlos can drive his new sports car from Raywood to Pigeon Hollow in $6\frac{2}{3}$ hours. If he has already driven $2\frac{3}{4}$ hours, *how much more* driving time *is left?*

1. The key words "how much more is left?" imply subtraction. Set up the problem with the larger whole number first.

$$6\frac{2}{3} - 2\frac{3}{4}$$

2. Find a common denominator for 3 and 4. Use their LCM, 12, for the common denominator.

3. $6\frac{2}{3} = 6\frac{8}{12}$ because $12 \div 3 = 4$ and $4 \times 2 = 8$; $2\frac{3}{4} = 2\frac{9}{12}$ because $12 \div 4 = 3$ and $3 \times 3 = 9$.

4. At this point, you have $6\frac{8}{12} - 2\frac{9}{12}$. In order to complete the subtraction, change the problem so that the first fraction is larger. You must subtract 1 whole from 6 to equal 5. The 1 whole that you subtracted or borrowed here is equal to $\frac{12}{12}$. The first fraction already has $\frac{8}{12}$ so add $\frac{12}{12} + \frac{8}{12} = \frac{20}{12}$. Now $6\frac{8}{12} = 5\frac{20}{12}$.

5. The problem now looks like $5\frac{20}{12} - 2\frac{9}{12}$.

6. Subtract the whole numbers and the fractions.

$$5\frac{20}{12} - 2\frac{9}{12} = 3\frac{11}{12}$$

7. The answer is $3\frac{11}{12}$ hours.

Multiplication

Jodie bought 100 shares of stock in the Lucky Circle cereal company. The price was $16\frac{3}{4}$ *a share*. How much did Jodie pay for the stock (not counting commission or any other costs)?

1. There are no key words here, but multiplication is implied since the price for 1 share is given and you want to know the price for 100 shares. Multiply $100 \times 16\frac{3}{4}$.

2. Rewrite $16\frac{3}{4}$ as an improper fraction by multiplying $16 \cdot 4 = 64$ and adding 3, $64 + 3 = 67$. 67 is your numerator and 4 remains as your denominator, $16\frac{3}{4} = \frac{67}{4}$.

3. Now you can multiply $100 \cdot \frac{67}{4}$. Use canceling to divide 4 into 100 and 4 into itself, $\overset{25}{100} \cdot \frac{67}{4}_1$. Multiply $25 \cdot 67$. Your answer is $1675.

Division

Sima needs $\frac{1}{2}$ pound of ground turkey meat for each turkey burger she's making for the snack bar at the school fair. She has 16 pounds of turkey meat. How many turkey burgers can be made from the meat?

1. There are no key words here, but division is implied since the total pounds are stated, and the amount for each burger is also given.

2. Start with the larger number, $16 \div \frac{1}{2}$.

3. Invert the second number and change to a multiplication problem, $16 \cdot \frac{2}{1}$.

4. Multiply $16 \cdot 2$ and simplify.

5. In this case, $16 \cdot 2 = 32$ turkey burgers.

BRAIN TICKLERS
Set # 15

Solve these funtastic fraction word problems:
(Remember—Preview, View, Do, and Review!)

1. Douglas poured $3\frac{1}{2}$ cups of flour into his mixing bowl. If his chocolate chip cookie recipe calls for 5 cups of flour, *how much more* flour does he need?

2. Lisette has a piece of wood $12\frac{3}{4}$ feet long and wants to *divide* it into 3 shelves. How long will each shelf be?

3. Joan babysits 4 hours on Monday, $3\frac{1}{2}$ hours on Tuesday, $5\frac{1}{3}$ hours on Wednesday, 5 hours on Thursday, and $4\frac{1}{4}$ hours on Friday. How many hours does Joan babysit *altogether* for the 5 days?

4. Jesse can mow the lawn in 6 hours. It takes his brother Tim $\frac{3}{4}$ *of that time*. How long does it take Tim to mow the lawn?

5. Erica worked on her math homework for $\frac{7}{8}$ of an hour and her English homework for $\frac{3}{4}$ of an hour. For how many hours did Erica work on math and English *combined*?

6. Janice and Judy are twins. At birth, Judy weighed 7 pounds and Janice weighed $6\frac{5}{8}$ pounds. What was the *difference* in their weight?

7. Jordan's jeep travels $22\frac{1}{2}$ miles on *one* gallon of gasoline. How far can it travel on $4\frac{1}{2}$ gallons of gasoline?

8. Michael's mom bought a turkey that weighed $12\frac{3}{4}$ pounds for the holidays. After the skin and the breast bone were *removed*, the turkey weighed $10\frac{1}{2}$ pounds.

a) What was the weight of the skin and bone?

b) Into how many $\frac{1}{4}$ pound servings can Michael's mom *divide* the turkey?

9. After finishing his homework, Ethan sat down in front of his big screen TV to watch the football game. At the time, team A had $\frac{2}{7}$ *of the number of points* that team B had. If team B had 21 points, how many did team A have?

10. Rosalie was downloading her favorite songs from the Web onto her computer. She then burned the music onto CDs. She completed 2 CDs, $\frac{2}{3}$ of another, and $\frac{3}{5}$ of a fourth CD. In *total*, how many CDs contain music?

11. The Santiago family purchased stock in Smooth Airlines one year ago. Each share of stock was priced at $\$5\frac{1}{8}$. Today each share of stock is worth $\$7\frac{1}{2}$. How many dollars did each share of stock *increase*?

12. Mrs. Cohen's math class was weighing pounds of oranges in plastic bags. If the first bag had $12\frac{3}{8}$ pounds, the second had $20\frac{1}{4}$ pounds, and the third bag had $5\frac{7}{8}$ pounds, how many pounds were there *altogether*?

13. One chocolate candy bar weighs $\frac{3}{8}$ of a pound. How much do three candy bars weigh?

14. Monique used $4\frac{1}{2}$ cups of flour to make three strawberry shortcakes. How many cups of flour did she use in *each* strawberry shortcake?

15. Dayshaun wants to buy a sweater that is priced at $\frac{1}{4}$ off the regular price of $48.

    a) How much does he save with this discount?

    b) What is the sale price?

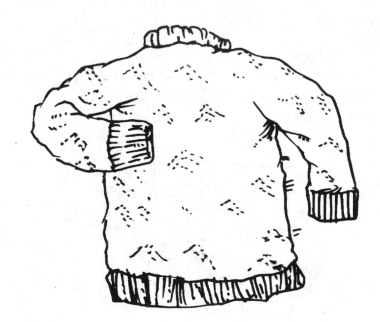

(Answers are on pages 177–185.)

BRAIN TICKLERS—THE ANSWERS

Set # 15, pages 173–176

Look for key words or phrases to make your work easier.

1. The phrase "how much more" gives a hint of subtraction. To find how much more flour, subtract the amount used from the total amount needed. The problem becomes $5 - 3\frac{1}{2}$. You must change the 5 into a mixed number so that you can subtract fractions. Here, subtract 1 from 5 to equal 4. The 1 whole that you borrowed is equal to $\frac{2}{2}$ because 2 is the denominator already in the problem. Since $5 = 4\frac{2}{2}$ and $3\frac{1}{2} = 3\frac{1}{2}$, the problem now looks like $4\frac{2}{2} - 3\frac{1}{2}$. Now subtract the whole numbers and the fractions, $4\frac{2}{2} - 3\frac{1}{2} = 1\frac{1}{2}$. The answer is $1\frac{1}{2}$ more cups of flour.

2. The word "divide" lets you know this is a division problem. Set your problem up with the larger whole number first, $12\frac{3}{4} \div 3$. Invert the 3 to its reciprocal and set up a multiplication problem, $12\frac{3}{4} \times \frac{1}{3}$. Change $12\frac{3}{4}$ to an improper fraction by multiplying 4 times 12 and adding 3, $4 \times 12 = 48$ and $48 + 3 = 51$. Keep your denominator of 4, so $12\frac{3}{4} = \frac{51}{4}$. The problem now looks like $\frac{51}{4} \times \frac{1}{3}$. Use canceling to divide 3 into 51 and 3 into 3, $\frac{\overset{17}{51}}{4} \times \frac{1}{\underset{1}{3}}$. Multiply the remaining numbers to get $\frac{17}{4}$. Divide 4 into 17 to get a mixed number answer of $4\frac{1}{4}$. Each shelf will be $4\frac{1}{4}$ feet long.

3. The word "altogether" implies addition. Add $4 + 3\frac{1}{2} + 5\frac{1}{3} + 5 + 4\frac{1}{4}$. You can add the whole numbers, $4 + 3 + 5 + 5 + 4 = 21$, and find a common denominator for the three fractions $\frac{1}{2}, \frac{1}{3},$ and $\frac{1}{4}$. The multiples of 2 are 2, 4, 6, 8, 10, 12 . . . , the multiples of 3 are 3, 6, 9, 12 . . . , and the multiples of 4 are 4, 8, 12 . . . . The LCM is 12. Rewrite $\frac{1}{2}$ with the common denominator of 12, $\frac{1}{2} = \frac{?}{12}$. Divide 2 into 12 and multiply the result by 1. The new result, 6, fills in the ?, so $\frac{1}{2} = \frac{6}{12}$. Similarly, $\frac{1}{3} = \frac{4}{12}$ and $\frac{1}{4} = \frac{3}{12}$. Your fractions now look like $\frac{6}{12} + \frac{4}{12} + \frac{3}{12}$. Add them to equal $\frac{13}{12}$. Put together the whole number answer and the fraction answer to equal $21\frac{13}{12}$. Change $\frac{13}{12}$ to $1\frac{1}{12}$ by dividing 12 into 13 with a fractional remainder. You now have $21 + 1\frac{1}{12}$. Add the whole numbers and bring along the fraction to equal $22\frac{1}{12}$ hours of babysitting for Joan.

4. The key words "of that time" imply multiplication, since you are finding a fractional part of a given amount. Multiply $6 \times \frac{3}{4}$. Use canceling to divide 2 into both 6 and 4, $\overset{3}{\cancel{6}} \times \frac{3}{\underset{2}{\cancel{4}}}$. Multiply the remaining numerators and denominators to get $\frac{9}{2}$. Change $\frac{9}{2}$ into a mixed number by dividing 2 into 9. The answer is $4\frac{1}{2}$. It takes Tim $4\frac{1}{2}$ hours to mow the lawn.

5. The word "combined" gives a hint of an addition problem. Add $\frac{7}{8}$ of an hour to $\frac{3}{4}$ of an hour, $\frac{7}{8} + \frac{3}{4}$. Find a common denominator for 8 and 4. The multiples of 8 are 8, 16 . . . , and the multiples of 4 are 4, 8, 12 . . . . The LCM, the common denominator, is 8. Change $\frac{3}{4}$ into $\frac{6}{8}$ by dividing 4 into 8 and multiplying the result by 3 to get 6, $\frac{3}{4} = \frac{6}{8}$. The fraction $\frac{7}{8}$ stays the same because it is already written with the common denominator. You now have $\frac{7}{8} + \frac{6}{8}$. Add the numerators to get $\frac{13}{8}$. Change $\frac{13}{8}$ to a mixed number by dividing 8 into 13 to get 1 with a fractional remainder of $\frac{5}{8}$. Erica worked on her math and English homework for a combined $1\frac{5}{8}$ hours.

6. The word "difference" is the key word for the answer to a subtraction problem. The difference in Janice and Judy's weight is the answer to $7 - 6\frac{5}{8}$. Change 7 into a mixed number with a fractional denominator of 8 so that you have two fractional parts to subtract. To do this, subtract 1 whole from the 7, making it a 6. In this problem, the 1 that you borrowed is equal to $\frac{8}{8}$. Since $7 = 6\frac{8}{8}$ and $6\frac{5}{8} = 6\frac{5}{8}$, the problem now looks like $6\frac{8}{8} - 6\frac{5}{8}$. Subtract the whole numbers and the fractions.

$$6\frac{8}{8} - 6\frac{5}{8} = \frac{3}{8}$$

The answer is $\frac{3}{8}$ of a pound difference in weight.

7. Since the number of miles for one gallon is given, multiply to find the number of miles for $4\frac{1}{2}$ gallons. The problem looks like $22\frac{1}{2} \times 4\frac{1}{2}$. Change $22\frac{1}{2}$ to an improper fraction by multiplying 2×22 and adding 1, $2 \times 22 = 44$ and $44 + 1 = 45$. Keep your denominator of 2, so $22\frac{1}{2} = \frac{45}{2}$. For $4\frac{1}{2}$, multiply 2×4 and add 1, $2 \times 4 = 8$ and $8 + 1 = 9$. Keep your denominator of 2, so $4\frac{1}{2} = \frac{9}{2}$. The problem now looks like $\frac{45}{2} \times \frac{9}{2}$. There are no common factors between the numerators and the denominators, $45 \times 9 = 405$ and $2 \times 2 = 4$. The answer as an improper fraction is $\frac{405}{4}$. Divide 4 into 405 to get the mixed number $101\frac{1}{4}$. Jordan's jeep can travel $101\frac{1}{4}$ miles on $4\frac{1}{2}$ gallons of gasoline.

8. a) From the word "removed," you get a hint of subtraction. Subtract the weight of the turkey after the trim from the weight of the turkey before the trim. This gives $12\frac{3}{4} - 10\frac{1}{2}$. The LCM of 4 and 2, your new common denominator, is 4. The mixed number $12\frac{3}{4}$ already has the new denominator of 4. For $10\frac{1}{2}$, divide 2 into 4 and multiply the resulting answer of 2 by the 1 in the numerator to get 2, $10\frac{1}{2} = 10\frac{2}{4}$. Now, subtract $12\frac{3}{4} - 10\frac{2}{4}$ to get $2\frac{1}{4}$. The total weight of the skin and breast bone was $2\frac{1}{4}$ pounds.

b) The key word "divide" refers to division. Take the current weight of the turkey, $10\frac{1}{2}$ pounds, and divide this weight by $\frac{1}{4}$, which is the weight of each serving, $10\frac{1}{2} \div \frac{1}{4}$. Change $10\frac{1}{2}$ into an improper fraction by multiplying 2×10 and adding $1, 2 \times 10 + 1 = 21$. This 21 becomes your numerator and 2 remains as your denominator to give $\frac{21}{2}$. Invert $\frac{1}{4}$ to its reciprocal of 4 and change the problem to multiplication, $\frac{21}{2} \times 4$. Divide 2 into both 2 and 4, $\frac{21}{\underset{1}{2}} \times 4\overset{2}{}$. Multiply the remaining numbers to get $\frac{42}{1}$. Your answer is 42. Michael's mom can divide the turkey into 42 servings.

9. The phrase "$\frac{2}{7}$ of the number of points that team B had" implies multiplication, since you are finding a fractional part of a given amount. The given amount is team B's score of 21. Multiply $\frac{2}{7} \times 21$. Use canceling to divide 7 into both 21 and itself, $\frac{2}{\underset{1}{7}} \times 21\overset{3}{}$. Multiply the remaining numerators to get 6. Team A had 6 points.

10. The word "total" refers to addition. Add $2 + \frac{2}{3} + \frac{3}{5}$ by finding a common denominator for 3 and 5. The multiples of 3 are 3, 6, 9, 12, 15 . . . , and the multiples of 5 are 5, 10, 15. . . . . The LCM, the common denominator, is 15. Rewrite $\frac{2}{3}$ by dividing 3 into 15 and multiplying the result by 2 to get $\frac{2}{3} = \frac{10}{15}$. Similarly, $\frac{3}{5} = \frac{9}{15}$. You now have $2 + \frac{10}{15} + \frac{9}{15}$. Add the two fractions to get $2 + \frac{19}{15}$. Change $\frac{19}{15}$ into a mixed number by dividing 15 into 19 to get 1 with a fractional remainder of $\frac{4}{15}$. So, $\frac{19}{15} = 1\frac{4}{15}$. You now have $2 + 1\frac{4}{15}$. Add the whole numbers and bring the fractional part along to get $3\frac{4}{15}$. Rosalie used $3\frac{4}{15}$ CDs.

11. To find the "amount of increase" subtract $5\frac{1}{8}$ from
    $7\frac{1}{2}$: $7\frac{1}{2} - 5\frac{1}{8}$. Find a common denominator by listing the
    multiples of 2: 2, 4, 6, 8, 10 . . . , and the multiples of 8:
    8, 16, 24 . . . . The LCM and the common denominator are 8.
    Rewrite $7\frac{1}{2}$ with the new denominator of 8, $7\frac{1}{2} = 7\frac{?}{8}$. Divide 2
    into 8 and multiply this answer of 4 by the 1 in the numerator
    to get 4, $7\frac{1}{2} = 7\frac{4}{8}$. $5\frac{1}{8}$ already has the common denominator,
    so subtract $7\frac{4}{8} - 5\frac{1}{8}$ to get $2\frac{3}{8}$. Each share of stock increased
    by $2\frac{3}{8}$ dollars.

12. The word "altogether" indicates addition. Add $12\frac{3}{8}$, $20\frac{1}{4}$, and
    $5\frac{7}{8}$. In order to find a common denominator, list multiples of
    4: 4, 8, 12, 16 . . . , and multiples of 8: 8, 16, 24, 32 . . . . The
    common denominator and LCM are 8. Rewrite $20\frac{1}{4}$ with the
    new denominator of 8, $20\frac{1}{4} = 20\frac{?}{8}$. Divide 4 into 8 and multi-
    ply the answer of 2 by 1, $20\frac{1}{4} = 20\frac{2}{8}$. The other fractions of
    $12\frac{3}{8}$ and $5\frac{7}{8}$ already have the common denominator. Now you
    can add $12\frac{3}{8} + 20\frac{2}{8} + 5\frac{7}{8}$. Add the whole numbers
    $12 + 20 + 5 = 37$, and the fractions, $\frac{3}{8} + \frac{2}{8} + \frac{7}{8} = \frac{12}{8}$.
    Change $\frac{12}{8}$ into $1\frac{4}{8} = 1\frac{1}{2}$ by dividing 8 into 12 and reducing
    to simplest form. The answer so far is $37 + 1\frac{1}{2}$. Add to get a
    final answer of $38\frac{1}{2}$ pounds.

13. Since the weight of one candy bar is given, multiply to find the weight of three candy bars. Multiply $3 \times \frac{3}{8}$.

    Treat your whole number 3 as if it were the numerator in $\frac{3}{1}$. Since there is no canceling, multiply the numerators and then the denominators, resulting in $\frac{9}{8}$.

    $$\frac{3}{1} \times \frac{3}{8} = \frac{9}{8}$$

    Change $\frac{9}{8}$ to a mixed number by dividing 9 by 8 resulting in $1\frac{1}{8}$.

    $$9 \div 8 = 1\frac{1}{8}$$

    Three candy bars weigh $1\frac{1}{8}$ pounds.

14. The word "each" implies division.

    Divide $4\frac{1}{2}$ by 3, $4\frac{1}{2} \div 3$.

    Now, multiply $4\frac{1}{2}$ by the reciprocal of 3,

    $$4\frac{1}{2} \times \frac{1}{3}.$$

    Change $4\frac{1}{2}$ to an improper fraction of $\frac{9}{2}$ and multiply by $\frac{1}{3}$, $\frac{9}{2} \times \frac{1}{3}$.

    Next, use canceling to divide 3 into 3 and 3 into 9,

    $$\frac{3\cancel{9}}{2} \times \frac{1}{\cancel{3}\,1}.$$

    Multiply what's left to get $\frac{3}{2}$. Change this improper fraction to $1\frac{1}{2}$ by dividing the denominator into the numerator.

    Monique used $1\frac{1}{2}$ cups of flour in each cake.

15. a) The phrase "$\frac{1}{4}$ off" implies multiplication since you want to find a part of a given amount. Multiply $\frac{1}{4}$ by 48. Treat 48 as if it were in the numerator of $\frac{48}{1}$. Then, use canceling to divide 4 into 4, resulting in 1, and 4 into 48, resulting in 12.

$$\frac{1}{\underset{1}{\cancel{4}}} \times \frac{\overset{12}{\cancel{48}}}{1}$$

Dayshaun saved $12 on his sweater.

b) Subtract $48 − $12. This equals a sale price of $36.

CHAPTER ELEVEN

Plenty of Practice

Here is more practice for you to do
Puzzles and problems and solutions, too.

EVEN MORE BRAIN TICKLERS

Solve each problem. Write in simplified form. Circle the correct answer. Check!

1. Reduce $\frac{20}{45}$ to simplest form.

   a) $\frac{5}{9}$ b) $\frac{4}{45}$ c) $\frac{4}{9}$ d) $\frac{10}{25}$

2. $4\frac{7}{8} + 7\frac{3}{4}$

   a) $11\frac{5}{8}$ b) $12\frac{5}{8}$ c) $11\frac{5}{16}$ d) $12\frac{3}{8}$

3. $3\frac{1}{2} \div 2$

   a) $1\frac{3}{4}$ b) $\frac{4}{7}$ c) $6\frac{1}{2}$ d) $1\frac{1}{2}$

4. $8 - 2\frac{3}{7}$

   a) $6\frac{3}{7}$ b) $6\frac{4}{7}$ c) $5\frac{5}{7}$ d) $5\frac{4}{7}$

5. $\left(\frac{3}{4}\right)^2 + \frac{1}{2} - \frac{1}{8}$

   a) $\frac{15}{16}$ b) $\frac{9}{8}$ c) $1\frac{1}{4}$ d) $2\frac{1}{2}$

6. Jim runs $1\frac{1}{2}$ miles on Monday, $2\frac{1}{3}$ miles on Tuesday, and $1\frac{5}{6}$ miles on Wednesday. How many miles did he run in all?

    a) $4\frac{5}{6}$ b) $5\frac{2}{3}$ c) $4\frac{1}{6}$ d) 5

7. Change $4\frac{5}{6}$ to an improper fraction.

    a) $\frac{17}{6}$ b) $\frac{180}{6}$ c) $\frac{36}{6}$ d) $\frac{29}{6}$

8. $5\frac{1}{3} \times 4\frac{1}{2}$

    a) $20\frac{1}{6}$ b) 22   c) 24   d) 23

9. $\left(\frac{1}{2}\right)^2 \times 4$

    a) $\frac{1}{4}$ b) 2   c) $\frac{1}{2}$ d) 1

10. $\frac{7}{8} \div 3$

    a) $\frac{7}{24}$ b) $\frac{21}{8}$ c) $\frac{29}{24}$ d) $\frac{24}{7}$

11. There are 584 attorneys at a convention.

   A) If $\frac{1}{4}$ of them are women, how many are women?

       a) 2336   b) 292   c) 144   d) 146

   B) How many are men?

       a) 438   b) 146   c) 242   d) 779

12. $\left(1\frac{1}{3} - \frac{2}{3}\right) \times \frac{3}{5}$

       a) $\frac{1}{5}$ b) 3   c) $\frac{2}{5}$ d) $\frac{2}{3}$

13. Rewrite $\frac{14}{3}$ as a mixed number.

       a) $4\frac{1}{3}$ b) $2\frac{3}{4}$ c) $3\frac{1}{4}$ d) $4\frac{2}{3}$

14. Which fraction is larger, $\frac{2}{3}$ or $\frac{8}{9}$?

       a) $\frac{8}{9}$ b) $\frac{2}{3}$

15. $\frac{3}{4} + 1\frac{7}{12}$

       a) $1\frac{11}{12}$ b) $2\frac{1}{3}$ c) $2\frac{7}{12}$ d) $2\frac{3}{8}$

16. If we have traveled $2\frac{1}{2}$ hours of a 6-hour trip, how many hours are left to travel?

       a) $5\frac{1}{2}$ b) $8\frac{1}{2}$ c) $4\frac{1}{2}$ d) $3\frac{1}{2}$

17. $\left(\frac{2}{3}\right)^3$

    a) $\frac{6}{9}$ b) $\frac{4}{9}$ c) $\frac{8}{27}$ d) $\frac{8}{3}$

18. Which fraction is larger, $\frac{1}{8}$ or $\frac{1}{9}$?

    a) $\frac{1}{9}$ b) $\frac{1}{8}$

19. 189 ounces of cereal will be equally separated into $4\frac{1}{2}$-ounce boxes. How many boxes of cereal will there be?

    a) 43   b) 42   c) 44   d) 50

20. Reduce $8\frac{16}{18}$ to simplest form.

    a) $8\frac{8}{9}$ b) $8\frac{2}{9}$ c) $8\frac{1}{8}$ d) $8\frac{6}{9}$

21. $15\frac{3}{5} - 11\frac{4}{5}$

    a) $3\frac{4}{5}$ b) $4\frac{1}{5}$ c) $4\frac{4}{5}$ d) $3\frac{1}{5}$

22. Maggie's gym class played volleyball for $\frac{1}{5}$ of the period, basketball for $\frac{1}{4}$ of the period, and jogged for $\frac{1}{6}$ of the period.

    A) What part of the gym period was spent on these activities?

        a) $\frac{13}{15}$ b) $\frac{37}{60}$ c) $\frac{25}{60}$ d) $\frac{39}{60}$

    B) What fractional part of the period is left over?

        a) $\frac{23}{60}$ b) $\frac{25}{60}$ c) $\frac{21}{60}$ d) $\frac{30}{60}$

23. There are 145 students going on a class trip.

    A) If $\frac{2}{5}$ of the class are female students, how many are female?

        a) 50   b) 58   c) 56   d) 78

    B) How many are male?

        a) 122   b) 58   c) 72   d) 87

24. $\frac{3}{4} = \frac{?}{28}$

    a) 7   b) 12   c) 14   d) 21

25. $\frac{3}{8} + 1\frac{1}{6} + 3\frac{5}{12}$

    a) $4\frac{23}{24}$ b) $4\frac{7}{12}$ c) $5\frac{1}{12}$ d) $4\frac{9}{24}$

26. $\frac{6}{11} - \frac{1}{3}$

    a) $\frac{7}{33}$ b) $\frac{5}{8}$ c) $\frac{5}{11}$ d) $\frac{17}{33}$

27. $\left(\frac{1}{2}\right)^2 - \frac{1}{4} \div 2$

    a) $\frac{1}{4}$ b) 2   c) $\frac{1}{8}$ d) $\frac{3}{8}$

28. Arrange in order from largest to smallest: $\frac{1}{6}, \frac{2}{9}, \frac{2}{3}$.

    a) $\frac{2}{3}, \frac{2}{9}, \frac{1}{6}$ b) $\frac{2}{3}, \frac{1}{6}, \frac{2}{9}$ c) $\frac{2}{9}, \frac{1}{6}, \frac{2}{3}$ d) $\frac{1}{6}, \frac{2}{9}, \frac{2}{3}$

29. $7\frac{6}{7} - 2\frac{3}{7}$

    a) $5\frac{7}{9}$ b) $9\frac{3}{7}$ c) $4\frac{3}{7}$ d) $5\frac{3}{7}$

30. Tim spends $\frac{1}{6}$ of his salary on entertainment and $\frac{1}{4}$ on clothes.

    A) What fraction of his salary does he spend on these two items?

    a) $\frac{5}{12}$ b) $\frac{1}{10}$ c) $\frac{1}{5}$ d) $\frac{1}{3}$

    B) What fractional part is left over for other things?

    a) $\frac{5}{12}$ b) $\frac{5}{6}$ c) $\frac{7}{12}$ d) $\frac{7}{10}$

31. Charla and Javier want to bake cupcakes for their youth group. They use 2 cups of flour for 24 cupcakes. At this same rate, how many cups of flour will be needed for 36 cupcakes?

    a) 5 cups   b) 3 cups   c) 2 cups   d) $3\frac{1}{2}$ cups

32. If 6 pounds of bananas cost $1.86, how much will 1 pound cost?

    a) $.62   b) $.93   c) $.31   d) $.98

33. Solve this proportion: $\frac{5}{6} = \frac{12}{n}$.

    a) $14\frac{2}{5}$ b) 18   c) 10   d) $14\frac{1}{4}$

34. Simplify this ratio: $\frac{28\ skiers}{42\ skiers}$.

    a) $\frac{2}{3}$ b) $\frac{6}{7}$ c) $\frac{4}{7}$ d) $\frac{7}{6}$

35. 160 high school freshmen attended the football game last Saturday. 240 sophomores attended the game.

    A) What was the ratio of freshmen to sophomores?

       a) $\frac{1}{12}$ b) $\frac{2}{3}$ c) $\frac{7}{12}$ d) $\frac{2}{5}$

    B) What was the ratio of freshmen to the total number of freshmen and sophomores?

       a) $\frac{1}{2}$ b) $\frac{1}{4}$ c) $\frac{2}{3}$ d) $\frac{2}{5}$

36. $\left(\frac{2}{5}\right)^3 (10) \left(\frac{1}{2}\right)$

    a) 2   b) $\frac{4}{5}$ c) $\frac{8}{25}$ d) 8

37. Paula played computer games for $3\frac{1}{2}$ hours on Friday night and $2\frac{1}{4}$ hours on Saturday. If her parents told her she could play for a total of 8 hours for the whole weekend (from Friday night through Sunday) how much more time does she still have to play on Sunday?

    a) $13\frac{3}{4}$ hours   b) $2\frac{1}{4}$ hours   c) $4\frac{1}{2}$ hours   d) $3\frac{3}{4}$ hours

38. $2\frac{1}{3} + \frac{3}{4} \times \frac{6}{7}$

    a) $2\frac{9}{14}$ b) $3\frac{78}{84}$ c) $3\frac{1}{4}$ d) $2\frac{41}{42}$

39. The space shuttle is scheduled to blast off from Cape Canaveral in Florida at 10:00 A.M. At 8:30 A.M., an announcement from the Space Center says the shuttle will be delayed $\frac{3}{4}$ of an hour. At 8:45 A.M. another announcement delays the blast off time for an additional $1\frac{1}{2}$ hours. At what time is it scheduled to blast off now?

    a) 11:15 A.M.   b) 10:45 A.M.   c) 12:15 P.M.   d) 12 noon

40. Mr. Johannsen has a cell phone plan with 1000 free anytime minutes a month. He used $\frac{2}{5}$ of his minutes the first half of the month.

    A) How many minutes did he use so far?

        a) 400   b) 600   c) 800   d) 200

    B) How many free anytime minutes does he have left for the rest of the month?

        a) 200   b) 600   c) 400   d) 800

41. Ricky bought 3 pounds of oranges for $2.96 at A & S Convenience Store, while Marty bought 5 pounds of oranges for $4.85 at Peppy's Market. Which boy paid less per pound?

    a) Ricky   b) Marty

42. Melu won $500 in a contest. He spent $170 on a smartphone and some clothes. He wanted to give part of the remaining money to charity and save the rest.

    A) After his spending, if he wanted to equally split $\frac{2}{3}$ of the remaining money among 4 charities, how much would each charity get?

       a) $330   b) $110   c) $55   d) $220

    B) After giving to charity, how much would be left for savings?

       a) $220   b) $110   c) $55   d) $330

43. On an airline flight to Florida, a preferred seat costs $1\frac{1}{2}$ times the cost of a regular seat. If a regular seat costs $22, how much is a preferred seat?

       a) $28.50   b) $33   c) $23.50   d) $36

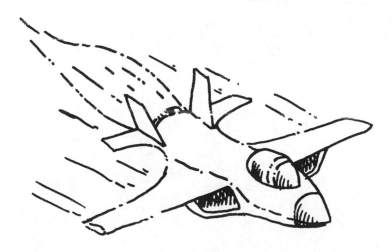

44. The cafeteria is running 2 specials on weekdays. Meal special A costs $4.44 and consists of 2 hot dogs, chips, an apple, and a medium drink. Meal special B consists of chips, an apple, and a medium drink, but only includes 1 hot dog. It sells for $\frac{2}{3}$ of the price of meal special A. What is the cost of meal special B?

   a) $6.10   b) $2.96   c) $3.99   d) $3.66

45. 276 boys and girls attend Jubilee Summer Camp. At this camp you can choose one sport to participate in each week.

   A) If $\frac{1}{2}$ choose baseball as their sport for the first week, how many children choose baseball for week 1?

   a) 184   b) 92   c) 112   d) 138

   B) If $\frac{3}{4}$ choose swimming for the second week, how many children did not choose swimming for week 2?

   a) 128   b) 69   c) 207   d) 75

   (Answers are on pages 211–226.)

GOING ON A PICNIC

The Gonzales Family is going on a summer picnic with 10 family members. Their shopping list includes the following items:

$\frac{1}{4}$ lb salami

$\frac{2}{3}$ lb bologna

$\frac{3}{4}$ lb turkey

$1\frac{1}{2}$ lb corned beef

$\frac{1}{2}$ lb pastrami

$1\frac{1}{3}$ lb roast beef

$1\frac{1}{4}$ lb potato salad

$2\frac{2}{3}$ lb cole slaw

2 dozen rolls (24)

$2\frac{1}{2}$ lb fruit salad

3 lb cookies

1. If the number of family members changes to 20, how would you adjust each item on the shopping list?

2. If the number of family members changes to 30, how would you adjust each item on the shopping list?

3. If only 5 of the original family members attend the picnic, how would you adjust the amount of each item on the shopping list?

(Answers are on pages 227–228.)

PUZZLING FRACTIONS #1

Why is a numerator like an elevator?

Multiply or divide to solve each problem below. Then find your answer in the column on the right and notice the letter next to it. Below, write this letter above the line that corresponds to the number of the question. When completed, you will have the answer to the riddle. The first one is done for you. All answers are in simplest form.

1. $\frac{3}{5} \times \frac{1}{2} = \frac{3}{10} = $ O

5. $7\frac{5}{6} \times 2$

2. $1\frac{1}{2} \times \frac{1}{4}$

6. $\frac{4}{9} \div \frac{2}{5}$

3. $5 \div \frac{1}{3}$

7. $10\frac{2}{3} \div \frac{1}{9}$

4. $16\frac{1}{2} \div 2\frac{2}{3}$

8. $4\frac{3}{8} \times 2\frac{3}{5}$

E	$6\frac{3}{16}$
T	$15\frac{2}{3}$
G	96
O	$\frac{3}{10}$
H	$11\frac{3}{8}$
P	$1\frac{1}{9}$
Y	$\frac{3}{8}$
B	15

$\overline{\ \ }\overline{\ \ }\overline{\ \ }\overline{\ \ }$ $\overline{\ \ }\overline{O}\overline{\ \ }\overline{\ \ }$ $\overline{\ \ }\overline{O}\ \overline{\ \ }\overline{O}$ $\overline{\ \ }\overline{\ \ }\overline{\ \ }$ $\overline{\ \ }\overline{O}\overline{\ \ }$!

5 8 4 2   3 1 5 8   7 1   5 1   5 8 4   5 1 6

(Answers are on page 229).

PUZZLING FRACTIONS #2

Why is a comb like a fraction?

Add or subtract to solve each problem below. Then find your answer in the column on the right and notice the letter next to it. On the next page, write this letter above the line that corresponds to the number of the question. When completed, you will have the answer to the riddle. The first problem is done for you. All answers are in simplest form.

1.
$$\frac{5}{6} = \frac{5}{6}$$
$$+ \frac{1}{3} = \frac{2}{6}$$
$$\overline{\frac{7}{6} = 1\frac{1}{6} = P}$$

2.
$$7\frac{1}{2}$$
$$- 2\frac{3}{4}$$
$$\overline{}$$

3.
$$2\frac{3}{8}$$
$$+ \frac{3}{5}$$
$$\overline{}$$

E $3\frac{1}{6}$

T $19\frac{1}{5}$

H 1

K $10\frac{2}{7}$

A $4\frac{3}{4}$

O $\frac{2}{5}$

R $16\frac{1}{5}$

B $10\frac{1}{3}$

Y $2\frac{39}{40}$

M $13\frac{1}{3}$

P $1\frac{1}{6}$

4. 6

$+ 4\frac{1}{3}$

_____

8. $\frac{8}{15}$

$- \frac{2}{15}$

_____

5. 8

$- 4\frac{5}{6}$

_____

9. $7\frac{2}{7}$

$+ 3$

_____

6. $7\frac{9}{10}$

$+ 11\frac{3}{10}$

_____

10. $16\frac{5}{6}$

$- 3\frac{1}{2}$

_____

7. $\frac{3}{7}$

$+ \frac{4}{7}$

_____

11. $12\frac{2}{5}$

$+ 3\frac{4}{5}$

_____

__ __ __ __   __ __ __ __   __ __ __ __   __ $\overset{\text{P}}{\underline{}}$ __ __ __!

6 7 5 3   4 8 6 7   10 2 9 5   2   1 2 11 6

(Answers are on page 229.)

PUZZLING FRACTIONS #3

What do a soldier and a math problem have in common?

Solve all problems below. Then find your answer in the column on the right and notice the letter next to it. Write this letter on each line at the bottom of page 205 that contains the number of that question. When completed, you will have the answer to the riddle. The first one is done for you. All answers are in simplest form.

1. $\frac{5}{9} + \frac{1}{2} = \frac{10}{18} + \frac{9}{18} = \frac{19}{18} = 1\frac{1}{18} = $ N

2. $3\frac{1}{4} \div \frac{1}{8}$

A $\quad 2\frac{1}{8}$

B $\quad 21\frac{37}{40}$

D $\quad \frac{5}{18}$

E $\quad \frac{1}{16}$

3. $10 - 3\frac{2}{5}$

4. $\left(\frac{3}{5}\right)^2 + \frac{1}{5}$

5. $2\frac{3}{7} \times \frac{7}{8}$

6. $18\frac{4}{5} + 3\frac{1}{8}$

7. $6 \times \frac{3}{4}$

8. $\frac{6}{18} - \frac{1}{18}$

9. $12 \div \frac{1}{5}$

10. $1\frac{1}{4} - \left(\frac{2}{3} - \frac{1}{3}\right)$

F $\frac{11}{12}$

H   456

L $1\frac{1}{2}$

N $1\frac{1}{18}$

O $\frac{14}{25}$

R   26

T   60

W $4\frac{1}{2}$

Y $6\frac{3}{5}$

11. At the end of a busy Saturday, Baker's Bakery had $\frac{1}{2}$ of a blueberry pie, $\frac{1}{4}$ of an apple pie, and $\frac{3}{4}$ of a pumpkin pie left. How much pie was left in total?

12. $\left(\frac{1}{4}\right)^3 \times 4$

13. There were 684 students at the Ridgewood High School football game. $\frac{2}{3}$ of the students were male. How many male students attended the game?

$\underset{\text{9 13 12 3}}{\_\ \_\ \_\ \_}$ $\underset{\text{6 4 9 13}}{\_\ \_\ \_\ \_}$ $\underset{\text{10 4 11 11 4 7}}{\_\ \_\ \_\ \_\ \_\ \_}$ $\underset{\text{5 1}}{\overset{\text{N}}{\_\ \_}}$ $\underset{\text{4 2 8 12 2}}{\_\ \_\ \_\ \_\ \_}!$

(Answers are on page 229.)

INCORRECT SOLUTIONS

Each of the following has an incorrect solution that is given.
Identify the mistake and correct the problem in each case.

1. $1\frac{3}{5} + 2\frac{3}{8}$

Incorrect solution: Add the whole numbers, the numerators,
and the denominators to get $3\frac{6}{13}$.

2. Find the LCM of 8 and 12.

Incorrect solution: 4 divides evenly into both 8 and 12, so 4 is
the LCM of 8 and 12.

3. $\frac{4}{5} \times \frac{10}{11}$

Incorrect solution: 5 divides evenly into both 5 and 10,

so $\frac{4}{5\cancel{5}} \times \frac{\cancel{10}^{\,2}}{11} = \frac{8}{55}$.

4. Joella read $\frac{5}{8}$ of her book over vacation. If her book had 576
   pages, how many pages did she read?

Incorrect solution: Since $\frac{5}{8} + \frac{3}{8} = 1$ whole book,
multiply $\frac{3}{8} \times 576$.

In $\frac{3}{8} \times 576$, 8 divides evenly into both 8 and 576, $\frac{3}{1\cancel{8}} \times \cancel{576}^{\,72}$, so
multiply 3 times 72 to get 216 pages.

5. Mrs. Livits buys cheese at the supermarket. She buys $\frac{3}{4}$ pound of sweet Muenster cheese, $\frac{1}{3}$ pound of Swiss cheese, and $1\frac{1}{2}$ pounds of American cheese. How much cheese did she buy altogether?

Incorrect solution: The LCD is 12 since 4, 3, and 2 all divide evenly into 12. Change each fraction into the new common denominator by dividing the old denominator into the new one and multiplying this answer by the old numerator. Then add the new numerators and put this answer over the LCD.

$$\frac{3}{4} = \frac{9}{12}, \frac{1}{3} = \frac{5}{12}, 1\frac{1}{2} = 1\frac{6}{12} \qquad \frac{9}{12} + \frac{5}{12} + 1\frac{6}{12} = 1\frac{20}{12}$$

Now, divide 12 into 20 to get $1\frac{8}{12}$. Simplify the mixed number to $1\frac{2}{3}$ since 4 divides evenly into both 8 and 12. Last, add $1\frac{2}{3}$ to the number 1 that is already there to get $2\frac{2}{3}$.

6. Jack is on a diet to lose $4\frac{1}{2}$ pounds a month. How many months will it take him to lose 36 pounds?

Incorrect solution: Divide 36 by $4\frac{1}{2}$ to find the number of months. Change $4\frac{1}{2}$ into an improper fraction by multiplying 2 by 4 and then putting this number over the original denominator of 2,

$$4\frac{1}{2} = \frac{8}{2}.$$

After this, you flip $\frac{8}{2}$ into its reciprocal of $\frac{2}{8}$ and multiply by 36,

$$36 \times \frac{2}{8}.$$

Since 4 divides evenly into both 8 and 36 you will have $\overset{9}{\cancel{36}} \times \frac{2}{\underset{2}{\cancel{8}}}$.

Then 2 divides evenly into both 2s, so your problem becomes

$9 \times \frac{\overset{1}{\cancel{2}}}{\underset{1}{\cancel{2}}}$, which is equal to 9.

7. This year in April, $4\frac{1}{2}$ inches of rain fell in New Jersey. In May, $3\frac{1}{6}$ inches of rain fell, and in June, $1\frac{7}{8}$ inches of rain fell in New Jersey.

a) How many inches of rain fell during these 3 months of the year?

b) If 15 inches of rain fell during these 3 months last year in New Jersey, how much less rain fell this year?

Incorrect solution: a) Here the common denominator is 16, so change each fraction to this new denominator, $4\frac{1}{2} = 4\frac{8}{16}$, $3\frac{1}{3} = 3\frac{3}{16}$, and $1\frac{7}{8} = 1\frac{14}{16}$. Now add $4\frac{8}{16} + 3\frac{3}{16} + 1\frac{14}{16}$ to get $8\frac{15}{16}$ inches.

b) Subtract $8\frac{15}{16}$ from 15. Change 15 into $14\frac{16}{16}$ and subtract $8\frac{15}{16}$ from $14\frac{16}{16}$, $14\frac{16}{16} - 8\frac{15}{16} = 6\frac{1}{16}$. The answer is $6\frac{1}{16}$ inches.

8. $11\frac{1}{4} - 8\frac{1}{2}$.

Incorrect solution: The LCD is 4 so change the fraction $\frac{1}{2}$ into $\frac{2}{4}$. The problem now reads $11\frac{1}{4} - 8\frac{2}{4}$.

Now subtract $\frac{2}{4} - \frac{1}{4}$ and $11 - 8$ to get an answer of $3\frac{1}{4}$.

9. Set up a proportion and solve:

Mr. Timpkins paid $127.50 for 15 hours of parking at the short-term parking lot at the airport. At this rate, what is the total parking charge for 20 hours?

Incorrect solution: Set up the proportion as

$$\frac{\text{total price}}{\text{number of hours}} = \frac{\text{total price}}{\text{number of hours}}$$

$$\frac{127.50}{20} = \frac{p}{15}$$

Multiply the cross products to get $20p - \$127.50 \times 15$ or $20p = \$1912.50$. Divide 20 into $1912.50 to get an answer of $95.63.

10. Use exponent rules to simplify: $\left(\frac{1}{3}\right)^3 \left(\frac{2}{9}\right) 3^2$.

Incorrect solution: Expand the problem to look like

$$\frac{1}{3} \times \frac{1}{3} \times \frac{1}{3} \times \frac{2}{9} \times 3 \times 3.$$

Cancel the 3s from the numerator with the 3s from the

denominator, $\frac{1}{1\cancel{3}} \times \frac{1}{1\cancel{3}} \times \frac{1}{1\cancel{3}} \times \frac{2}{9} \times \cancel{3}^{1} \times \cancel{3}^{1}$.

Multiply the remaining numerators and denominators $\frac{1 \times 1 \times 2}{9}$, to equal $\frac{2}{9}$.

(Answers are on pages 230–232.)

WORD SEARCH

Find these words in the following table of letters below:

Denominator
Numerator
Multiply
Divide
Add
Subtract
Cancel
Simplify
Fraction
Reciprocal
Ratio
Factor

D	S	S	R	O	T	C	A	F	D	R
I	R	I	U	O	P	A	T	A	N	O
L	N	M	M	B	I	T	R	N	U	T
A	C	P	O	M	T	O	A	O	M	A
C	D	L	T	I	A	R	C	I	E	N
O	E	I	R	N	N	R	A	T	R	I
R	O	F	V	A	N	D	D	C	A	M
P	I	Y	A	I	S	A	A	A	T	O
I	T	S	I	T	D	N	M	R	O	N
C	A	D	E	D	C	E	P	F	R	E
E	R	D	M	E	V	L	U	C	T	D
R	E	Y	L	P	I	T	L	U	M	N

(Answers are on page 233.)

ANSWERS TO EVEN MORE
BRAIN TICKLERS, PAGES 189–198

1. Look for a number that divides evenly into both the numerator and denominator. Find the GCF if possible. Here, both 20
   and 45 are divisible by 5 (since they end in 5 or 0), $\frac{20 \div 5 = 4}{45 \div 5 = 9}$.
   Therefore, the reduced fraction is $\frac{4}{9}$. The answer is (c).

2. Find a common denominator for 8 and 4. The multiples of 8
   are 8, 16, 24, 32 . . . , and the multiples of 4 are 4, 8, 12, 16, 20,
   24 . . . . The LCM is 8. The fraction $4\frac{7}{8}$ stays the same because
   the denominator is already 8. Rewrite $7\frac{3}{4}$ with an equivalent
   fraction with a denominator of 8 by dividing 8 by 4 to get 2,
   and then multiplying this 2 by the 3 in the numerator to
   get 6. The equivalent mixed number is $7\frac{6}{8}$. The problem now
   looks like $4\frac{7}{8} + 7\frac{6}{8}$. Add the two whole numbers, $4 + 7 = 11$.
   Add the two fractions, $\frac{7}{8} + \frac{6}{8} = \frac{13}{8}$. You now have $11\frac{13}{8}$.
   Divide 13 by 8 to get $1\frac{5}{8}$. Add $1\frac{5}{8}$ to the whole number 11 to
   get $11 + 1\frac{5}{8} = 12\frac{5}{8}$. The answer is (b).

3. Change $3\frac{1}{2}$ into an improper fraction by multiplying the denominator by the whole number and adding the numerator,
   $2 \times 3 + 1 = 7$. Put the 7 over the 2 to form the fraction $\frac{7}{2}$.
   Now invert the 2 after the ÷ symbol to its reciprocal of $\frac{1}{2}$,
   and change the division symbol into multiplication to look
   like $\frac{7}{2} \times \frac{1}{2}$. Multiply the numerators and denominators to get
   $\frac{7}{4}$. Divide 7 by 4 to get $1\frac{3}{4}$. The answer is (a).

4. In order to subtract $2\frac{3}{7}$ from 8, you must subtract 1 from 8 to equal 7. In this case, the 1 whole is traded for $\frac{7}{7}$. The problem now looks like $7\frac{7}{7} - 2\frac{3}{7}$. Subtract the two whole numbers, $7 - 2 = 5$ and the two fractions, $\frac{7}{7} - \frac{3}{7} = \frac{4}{7}$. Your answer is $5\frac{4}{7}$. The answer is (d).

5. This problem uses the order of operations PEMDAS. The exponent 2 tells you to square the $\frac{3}{4}$: $\frac{3}{4} \times \frac{3}{4} = \frac{9}{16}$. Now the problem looks like $\frac{9}{16} + \frac{1}{2} - \frac{1}{8}$. Find a common denominator for all three fractions at once. The multiples of 16 are 16, 32, 48 . . . , the multiples of 2 are 2, 4, 6, 8, 10, 12, 14, 16 . . . , and the multiples of 8 are 8, 16, 24 . . . . So, 16 is your LCM and your common denominator. The fraction $\frac{9}{16}$ stays the same since 16 is already your common denominator. Change $\frac{1}{2}$ to $\frac{8}{16}$ by dividing the two denominators, $16 \div 2 = 8$, and then multiplying by the numerator of 1, $8 \times 1 = 8$. Therefore, $\frac{1}{2} = \frac{8}{16}$. Change $\frac{1}{8}$ to $\frac{2}{16}$ by dividing the two denominators, $16 \div 8 = 2$, and then multiplying by the numerator of 1, $2 \times 1 = 2$, to get $\frac{1}{8} = \frac{2}{16}$. The problem now looks like $\frac{9}{16} + \frac{8}{16} - \frac{2}{16}$. Add the numerators $9 + 8 = 17$ and then subtract the numerator 2, $17 - 2 = 15$. Your answer is $\frac{15}{16}$. The answer is (a).

6. The phrase "in all" indicates addition. Add $1\frac{1}{2} + 2\frac{1}{3} + 1\frac{5}{6}$ by using a common denominator of 6. Rewrite $1\frac{1}{2}$ with the new common denominator of 6 by dividing the denominators, $6 \div 2 = 3$, and multiplying this 3 by the 1 in the numerator to get $1\frac{1}{2} = 1\frac{3}{6}$. Next, rewrite $2\frac{1}{3}$ with a denominator of 6 by dividing 6 by 3 to get 2 and then multiplying this 2 by the 1 in

the numerator to get $2\frac{1}{3} = 2\frac{2}{6}$. Finally, $1\frac{5}{6}$ stays the same because it already has a denominator of 6. The problem now looks like $1\frac{3}{6} + 2\frac{2}{6} + 1\frac{5}{6}$. Add all the whole numbers to equal 4 and all of the fractions to equal $\frac{10}{6}$. You now have $4\frac{10}{6}$. Rewrite $\frac{10}{6}$ as the mixed number $1\frac{4}{6}$ by dividing 10 by 6 and then reducing the fraction to get $1\frac{2}{3}$. Add $4 + 1\frac{2}{3}$ to get $5\frac{2}{3}$. The answer is (b).

7. Multiply the denominator by the whole number and add the numerator, $6 \times 4 + 5 = 29$. Put this number over the original denominator to get a fraction of $\frac{29}{6}$. The answer is (d).

8. Change both $5\frac{1}{3}$ and $4\frac{1}{2}$ into improper fractions. Multiply 3 by 5 and then add 1 to get 16. Put 16 over 3 to get $\frac{16}{3}$. Multiply 2 by 4 and then add 1 to get $8 + 1 = 9$. Put 9 over 2 to get $\frac{9}{2}$. The problem now looks like $\frac{16}{3} \times \frac{9}{2}$. You can cancel in both diagonal directions. Both 16 and 2 are divisible by 2, $16 \div 2 = 8$ and $2 \div 2 = 1$. Both 3 and 9 are divisible by 3, $9 \div 3 = 3$ and $3 \div 3 = 1$. The problem now looks like $\frac{8}{1} \times \frac{3}{1}$. Multiply 8×3 to get 24. The answer is (c).

9. Expand $\left(\frac{1}{2}\right)^2$ to $\frac{1}{2} \times \frac{1}{2}$. Multiply the numerators and denominators to get $\frac{1}{4}$. Then multiply $\frac{1}{4} \times 4$. Cancel by dividing 4 into the denominator of 4 and into the whole number 4, $4 \div 4 = 1$. The problem now looks like $\frac{1}{1} \times 1$. The answer is 1 or (d).

10. Change the 3 to its reciprocal of $\frac{1}{3}$. Also change $\div$ to $\times$. The problem now looks like $\frac{7}{8} \times \frac{1}{3}$. Multiply the numerators and denominators to get $\frac{7}{24}$. The answer is (a).

11. A) The word "of" often indicates multiplication with fractions. Here, multiply $\frac{1}{4} \times 584$. Cancel by dividing 4 into 4 and 584. The problem now looks like $\frac{1}{1} \times 146$ or 146. The answer is (d).

B) Since there are 584 attorneys altogether, subtract the number of women from 584 to equal the number of men. Here, $584 - 146 = 438$. There are 438 men. The answer is (a).

12. The order of operations tells you to perform the operations inside parentheses first. Since $1\frac{1}{3}$ and $\frac{2}{3}$ have the same denominator, you can subtract without changing denominators, but you must change the fractions so that the first fraction is larger than the second. There are two ways to do this. One way is to rewrite $1\frac{1}{3}$ as the improper fraction $\frac{4}{3}$. Then subtract, $\frac{4}{3} - \frac{2}{3} = \frac{2}{3}$. The other way is to represent 1 as $\frac{3}{3}$ and add this $\frac{3}{3}$ to the $\frac{1}{3}$ that's already there, $\frac{3}{3} + \frac{1}{3} = \frac{4}{3}$. Then subtract, $\frac{4}{3} - \frac{2}{3} = \frac{2}{3}$. The quantity inside the parentheses is $\frac{2}{3}$. Next, multiply $\frac{2}{3} \times \frac{3}{5}$. Use canceling to divide 3 into both 3s in the diagonal direction, $3 \div 3 = 1$. The problem now looks like $\frac{2}{1} \times \frac{1}{5}$. Multiply the numerators and denominators to get $\frac{2}{5}$. The answer is (c).

13. Divide 3 into 14. You get a whole number of 4 with a remainder of 2. This 2 becomes your numerator, and the divisor of 3 becomes your denominator to form the mixed number $4\frac{2}{3}$. The answer is (d).

14. To see which fraction is larger, cross multiply your two diagonals from bottom to top, $\overset{18}{}\frac{2}{3} \times \overset{24}{}\frac{8}{9}$ to get $9 \times 2 = 18$ and $3 \times 8 = 24$. Since 24 is larger than 18, the fraction $\frac{8}{9}$ is larger than the fraction $\frac{2}{3}$. The answer is (a).

15. Find a common denominator (LCM) for 4 and 12. The multiples of 4 are 4, 8, 12, 16 . . . , and the multiples of 12 are 12, 24, 36 . . . . The LCM, which is the common denominator for 4 and 12, is 12. Rewrite $\frac{3}{4}$ with a denominator of 12, $\frac{3}{4} = \frac{?}{12}$. Divide 4 into 12 and get 3 and then multiply this by the 3 in the numerator to get $\frac{3}{4} = \frac{9}{12}$. Because $1\frac{7}{12}$ already has the common denominator, it stays the same. The problem now looks like $\frac{9}{12} + 1\frac{7}{12}$. The whole number is 1. Add the two fractions, $\frac{9}{12} + \frac{7}{12} = \frac{16}{12}$. You now have $1\frac{16}{12}$. Change the $\frac{16}{12}$ into $1\frac{4}{12}$. You now have $1 + 1\frac{4}{12}$. Add the two whole numbers, $1 + 1 = 2$. You now have $2\frac{4}{12}$. Reduce $\frac{4}{12}$ to simplest form by dividing both 4 and 12 by 4, $4 \div 4 = 1$ and $12 \div 4 = 3$, to get a fraction of $\frac{1}{3}$. You now have $2\frac{1}{3}$. The answer is (b).

16. The phrase "are left" indicates subtraction. Your problem will look like $6 - 2\frac{1}{2}$. Subtract 1 from the 6 and change this into $\frac{2}{2}$ because 2 is the denominator in the original problem, and $\frac{2}{2}$ is equal to 1. Your problem now looks like $5\frac{2}{2} - 2\frac{1}{2}$. Subtract the two whole numbers and the two fractions, $5 - 2 = 3$ and $\frac{2}{2} - \frac{1}{2} = \frac{1}{2}$, to get an answer of $3\frac{1}{2}$. The answer is (d).

17. $\frac{2}{3}$ raised to the third power or "cubed" means to multiply $\frac{2}{3}$ by itself 3 times, $\frac{2}{3} \times \frac{2}{3} \times \frac{2}{3}$. Since there is no canceling, multiply the numerators and the denominators, $2 \times 2 \times 2 = 8$ and $3 \times 3 \times 3 = 27$. Your fraction is now $\frac{8}{27}$. Since this fraction is in simplest form (no number divides evenly into both the numerator and denominator), the answer is (c).

18. To see which fraction is larger, cross multiply your two diagonals from bottom to top, $\overset{9}{\frac{1}{8}} \times \overset{18}{\frac{1}{9}}$, $9 \times 1 = 9$ and $8 \times 1 = 8$. Since 9 is larger than 8, the fraction $\frac{1}{8}$ is larger than the fraction $\frac{1}{9}$. Also, when two fractions have 1 as their numerator, the one with the smaller denominator is the larger fraction. The answer is (b).

19. The phrase "separated into" gives the hint of division. Your problem will look like $189 \div 4\frac{1}{2}$. Change $4\frac{1}{2}$ to an improper fraction by multiplying 2 by 4 and adding 1 to get 9. Put the 9 over the original denominator to get $\frac{9}{2}$. Invert $\frac{9}{2}$ to $\frac{2}{9}$. Then change your problem to multiplication. It now looks like $189 \times \frac{2}{9}$. Cancel by dividing 9 into 189 and into 9, $189 \div 9 = 21$ and $9 \div 9 = 1$. The problem now looks like $21 \times \frac{2}{1}$. Multiply 21×2 to get 42. The answer is (b).

20. To reduce $\frac{16}{18}$, look for a common factor that divides evenly into both 16 and 18. It is best to find the greatest common factor (GCF). The factors of 16 are 2, 4, 6, 8, 16, and the factors of 18 are 2, 3, 6, 9, 18. The GCF is 2. Divide both 16 and 18 by 2, $16 \div 2 = 8$ and $18 \div 2 = 9$. The reduced fraction is $\frac{8}{9}$. Bring along the whole number 8 to your answer. You now have $8\frac{8}{9}$. The answer is (a).

21. Since the denominators are the same, you do not have to find a common denominator. However, since the second fraction is larger than the first, you must change the first fraction so that its numerator is larger than the second. Subtract 1 from 15 to equal 14. In this case, the 1 is traded for $\frac{5}{5}$, since 5 is the denominator in the problem. Add this $\frac{5}{5}$ to the $\frac{3}{5}$ that is already there, $\frac{5}{5} + \frac{3}{5} = \frac{8}{5}$. The problem now looks like $14\frac{8}{5} - 11\frac{4}{5}$. Subtract the two whole numbers, $14 - 11 = 3$. Subtract the two fractions, $\frac{8}{5} - \frac{4}{5} = \frac{4}{5}$. The answer is $3\frac{4}{5}$, or (a).

22. A) Since three activities with three fractions are mentioned, the problem lends itself to addition. The fractions should be "totaled" even though the word "total" isn't mentioned. The fractions of $\frac{1}{5} + \frac{1}{4} + \frac{1}{6}$ need a common denominator in order to be added. The multiples of 5 are 5, 10, 15, 20, 25, 30, 35, 40, 45, 50, 55, 60 . . . , the multiples of 4 are 4, 8, 12, 16, 20, 24, 28, 32, 36, 40, 44, 48, 52, 56, 60 . . . , and the multiples of 6 are 6, 12, 18, 24, 30, 36, 42, 48, 54, 60 . . . . The LCM is 60. Rewrite $\frac{1}{5}$ as $\frac{?}{60}$ by dividing 60 by 5 to get 12 and then multiplying 12 by the 1 in the numerator to get 12. The equivalent fraction is $\frac{12}{60}$. Rewrite $\frac{1}{4}$ as $\frac{?}{60}$ by dividing 60 by 4 to get 15 and then multiplying 15 by the 1 in the numerator to get 15. The equivalent fraction is $\frac{15}{60}$. Rewrite $\frac{1}{6}$ as $\frac{?}{60}$ by dividing 60 by 6 to get 10 and then multiplying 10 by the 1 in the numerator to get 10. The equivalent fraction is $\frac{10}{60}$. The problem now looks like $\frac{12}{60} + \frac{15}{60} + \frac{10}{60}$. Add the numerators to get $\frac{37}{60}$. The answer is (b).

B) The phrase "left over" implies subtraction. When you talk about fractional parts, all of your parts must add up to 1. To find the part left over, you find the difference between 1 and $\frac{37}{60}$. Here, one whole is equal to $\frac{60}{60}$. Subtract $\frac{60}{60} - \frac{37}{60}$ to get $\frac{23}{60}$. The answer is (a).

23. A) Looking at the phrase "$\frac{2}{5}$ of the class," you are asked to find a fractional part of a given amount, which indicates multiplication. Here the part is $\frac{2}{5}$ females and the given amount is 145, so you multiply $\frac{2}{5} \cdot 145$. Use canceling to divide 5 into 145 and into itself, $5 \div 5 = 1$ and $145 \div 5 = 29$. The problem now looks like $\frac{2}{1} \cdot 29$. Multiply $2 \cdot 29$ to equal 58. So, 58 students are female. The answer is (b).

B) The easiest way to find the number of males is to subtract the number of females from the total number of students, $145 - 58 = 87$. There are 87 males. The answer is (d).

24. Divide the denominator 4 into the denominator 28 to get 7. Multiply this 7 by the numerator 3 to get 21. Your new equivalent fraction is $\frac{21}{28}$, and the answer is 21, or (d).

25. Find a common denominator that 8, 6, and 12 all divide into evenly. The multiples of 8 are 8, 16, 24 . . . , the multiples of 6 are 6, 12, 18, 24 . . . , and the multiples of 12 are 12, 24 . . . . The common denominator, which is the least common multiple, is 24. Now, $\frac{3}{8} = \frac{9}{24}$ by dividing 8 into 24 to get 3 and multiplying this 3 by the numerator of 3 to get 9; $1\frac{1}{6} = 1\frac{4}{24}$ by dividing 6 into 24 to get 4 and multiplying this 4 by the numerator of 1 to get 4; and $3\frac{5}{12} = 3\frac{10}{24}$ by dividing 12 into 24

to get 2 and multiplying this 2 by the numerator of 5 to get 10. Your problem now looks like $\frac{9}{24} + 1\frac{4}{24} + 3\frac{10}{24}$. Add the whole numbers, $1 + 3 = 4$, and the numerators of your fractions, $\frac{9}{24} + \frac{4}{24} + \frac{10}{24} = \frac{23}{24}$. The answer is $4\frac{23}{24}$, or (a).

26. Find a common denominator that 11 and 3 divide into evenly. The multiples of 11 are $11, 22, 33, 44 \ldots$, and the multiples of 3 are $3, 6, 9, 12, 15, 18, 21, 24, 27, 30, 33 \ldots$. The least common multiple, the common denominator, is 33. Now, $\frac{6}{11} = \frac{18}{33}$ by dividing 11 into 33 to get 3 and multiplying this 3 by the numerator of 6 to get 18; and $\frac{1}{3} = \frac{11}{33}$ by dividing 3 into 33 to get 11 and multiplying this 11 by the numerator of 1 to get 11. The problem now looks like $\frac{18}{33} - \frac{11}{33}$. Subtract the numerators of your fractions to get $\frac{7}{33}$. The answer is (a).

27. According to the order of operations, $\left(\frac{1}{2}\right)^2$ would be simplified first as $\frac{1}{2} \times \frac{1}{2} = \frac{1}{4}$. Next, perform the division by inverting 2 to its reciprocal of $\frac{1}{2}$ and multiplying, $\frac{1}{4} \times \frac{1}{2}$. This result is $\frac{1}{8}$. The problem now looks like $\frac{1}{4} - \frac{1}{8}$. Find a common denominator for 4 and 8. The multiples of 4 are 4, 8, 12 . . . , and the multiples of 8 are 8, 16, 24 . . . . The LCM is 8. Use this for your common denominator. Now $\frac{1}{4} = \frac{2}{8}$ by dividing 4 into 8 to get 2 and multiplying this 2 by the 1 in the old numerator; and $\frac{1}{8}$ stays the same. The problem now looks like $\frac{2}{8} - \frac{1}{8}$. Subtract the numerators to get $\frac{1}{8}$ or (c).

28. To compare the size of fractions you must find a common denominator for all of the given fractions. The multiples of 6 are 6, 12, 18, 24 . . . , the multiples of 9 are 9, 18, 27 . . . , and the multiples of 3 are 3, 6, 9, 12, 15, 18 . . . . 18 is the LCM. Now, $\frac{1}{6} = \frac{3}{18}$ by dividing 6 into 18 to get 3 and multiplying this 3 by the numerator of 1 to get 3 as the new numerator; and $\frac{2}{9} = \frac{4}{18}$ by dividing 9 into 18 to get 2 and multiplying this 2 by the 2 in the old numerator; and $\frac{2}{3} = \frac{12}{18}$ by dividing 3 into 18 to get 6 and multiplying this 6 by the 2 in the old numerator to get 12 as the new numerator. Since $\frac{1}{6} = \frac{3}{18}, \frac{2}{9} = \frac{4}{18}$, and $\frac{2}{3} = \frac{12}{18}$, the largest fraction is $\frac{12}{18}$, or $\frac{2}{3}$. The next largest fraction is $\frac{4}{18}$, or $\frac{2}{9}$. The smallest fraction is $\frac{3}{18}$, or $\frac{1}{6}$. The fractions from largest to smallest are $\frac{2}{3}, \frac{2}{9}, \frac{1}{6}$, which is answer (a).

29. Since these two fractions already have a common denominator of 7, you can subtract your two fractions, $\frac{6}{7} - \frac{3}{7} = \frac{3}{7}$, and your two whole numbers, $7 - 2 = 5$. The answer is $5\frac{3}{7}$, or (d).

30. A) Since you do not know a salary amount, you can only work with the two fractions $\frac{1}{6}$ and $\frac{1}{4}$. Since the question mentions "on these two items," add $\frac{1}{6}$ and $\frac{1}{4}$ to find the fractional salary part spent. Find a common denominator. The multiples of 6 are 6, 12, 18 . . . , and the multiples of 4 are 4, 8, 12 . . . . The least common multiple, to use for the common denominator, is 12. Now $\frac{1}{6} = \frac{2}{12}$ by dividing 6 into 12 to get 2 and multiplying this 2 by the old numerator of 1 to get a new numerator of 2; and $\frac{1}{4} = \frac{3}{12}$ by dividing 4 into 12 to get 3 and multiplying this 3 by the old numerator of 1 to get a new numerator of 3. You now have $\frac{2}{12} + \frac{3}{12}$. Add to get $\frac{5}{12}$, or (a).

B) The words "left over" imply subtraction. When you talk about fractional parts, all of your parts must add up to 1 whole. To find the part left over, find the difference between 1 whole and $\frac{5}{12}$. Here, one whole is equal to $\frac{12}{12}$. Subtract $\frac{12}{12} - \frac{5}{12}$ to get $\frac{7}{12}$. The answer is (c).

31. Set up your problem as a proportion as follows: $\frac{cups\ of\ flour}{cupcakes} = \frac{cups\ of\ flour}{cupcakes}$. Replace the number of cups of flour and cupcakes from the problem into the appropriate places in your proportion: $\frac{2}{24} = \frac{c}{36}$ (2 cups of flour and 24 cupcakes go together and the unknown number of cups of flour c goes with 36 cupcakes). Multiply the cross products to get $24 \cdot c = 2 \cdot 36$, or $24c = 72$. Divide 24 into 72 to get an answer of 3. Therefore, at this rate, Charla and Javier would need 3 cups of flour for 36 cupcakes. This is equivalent to 2 cups of flour for 24 cupcakes. The correct answer is (b).

32. Since 1 pound indicates a unit rate, divide the number of pounds into the total price given to determine the unit price, or the price per pound $6\overline{)1.86}$ with 0.31 above. So, $.31 is the price for 1 pound of bananas. The correct answer is (c).

33. Multiply $5 \cdot n$ and set this equal to $6 \cdot 12$, $5n = 72$. Divide 5 into 72 to get an answer of $14\frac{2}{5}$. Therefore $n = 14\frac{2}{5}$. The correct answer is (a).

34. Look for a common factor, preferably the GCF, that will divide evenly into both 28 and 42. 7 is a common factor that will divide evenly into both 28 and 42. Use canceling to simplify, $\frac{28^4}{42_6}$. Now, you can use a common factor of 2 to simplify $\frac{4}{6}$ to $\frac{2}{3}$. From the beginning, if you had noticed that the GCF for 28 and 42 is 14, you could have simplified the fraction in one step $\frac{28^2}{42_3}$, by dividing 14 into both the numerator and denominator. The correct answer is (a).

35. A) Set up the ratio as $\frac{number\ of\ freshmen}{number\ of\ sophomores}$. The number of freshmen is equal to 160 and the number of sophomores is 240, so your fractional ratio becomes $\frac{160}{240}$. Since 80 is the GCF, divide both 160 and 240 by 80, $\frac{160^2}{240_3}$. Therefore the ratio of freshmen to sophomores is $\frac{2}{3}$. The correct answer is (b).

B) Set up the ratio as $\frac{number\ of\ freshmen}{total\ number\ of\ freshmen\ and\ sophomores}$. The total number of freshmen and sophomores is equal to $160 + 240 = 400$. The number of freshmen is 160, so $\frac{160}{400}$ is your fractional ratio. Since 160 and 400 are both divisible by 80, simplify to $\frac{160^2}{400_5}$. Therefore, the ratio of the number of freshmen to the total number of freshmen and sophomores is $\frac{2}{5}$. The correct answer is (d).

36. According to the order of operations, $\left(\frac{2}{5}\right)^3$ would be simpli-

    fied first as $\frac{2}{5} \times \frac{2}{5} \times \frac{2}{5} = \frac{8}{125}$. Now the problem looks like

    $\frac{8}{125}(10)\left(\frac{1}{2}\right)$. Write 10 as $\frac{10}{1}$. Use canceling to divide 2 into

    10 and itself, $\frac{8}{125}\left(\frac{^5\cancel{10}}{1}\right)\left(\frac{1}{\cancel{2}_1}\right)$. The problem now looks like

    $\frac{8}{125}\left(\frac{5}{1}\right)\left(\frac{1}{1}\right)$. Now use canceling to divide 5 into both 5 and

    125, $\frac{8}{_{25}\cancel{125}}\left(\frac{^1\cancel{5}}{1}\right)\left(\frac{1}{1}\right)$. The problem now looks like $\frac{8}{25}\left(\frac{1}{1}\right)\left(\frac{1}{1}\right)$.

    Multiply to get an answer of $\frac{8}{25}$. The answer is (c).

37. Add the time for Friday night, $3\frac{1}{2}$ hours, to the time for

    Saturday, $2\frac{1}{4}$ hours. Use the common denominator of 4, and

    change $3\frac{1}{2} = 3\frac{?}{4}$. Divide 2 into 4 and get 2, then multiply by

    the 1 in the numerator to get $3\frac{1}{2} = 3\frac{2}{4}$. Because $2\frac{1}{4}$ has the

    common denominator, it stays the same. Now add $3\frac{2}{4} + 2\frac{1}{4}$ to

    get $5\frac{3}{4}$ hours. Then subtract $5\frac{3}{4}$ from 8 to see how many

    hours are left for Sunday, $8 - 5\frac{3}{4}$. Subtract 1 from 8 and

    change it to $7\frac{4}{4}$ because 4 is the denominator in the original

    problem, and $\frac{4}{4}$ is equal to 1. Your problem now looks like

    $7\frac{4}{4} - 5\frac{3}{4}$. Subtract the two whole numbers and the two frac-

    tions, $7 - 5 = 2$ and $\frac{4}{4} - \frac{3}{4} = \frac{1}{4}$, to get an answer of $2\frac{1}{4}$ hours.

    The answer is (b).

38. According to the order of operations, multiply $\frac{3}{4} \times \frac{6}{7}$ first. Use canceling to divide 2 into both 4 and 6, $\frac{3}{{}_2 4} \times \frac{6^3}{7}$. It will now look like $\frac{3}{2} \times \frac{3}{7}$. Multiply the remaining numbers to get $\frac{9}{14}$. Now add $2\frac{1}{3} + \frac{9}{14}$. The multiples of 3 are 3, 6, 9, 12, 15, 18, 21, 24, 27, 30, 33, 36, 39, 42, 45 . . . , and the multiples of 14 are 14, 28, 42, 56 . . . . The LCM, which is the lowest common denominator of 3 and 14, is 42. Rewrite $2\frac{1}{3}$ with a common denominator of 42, $2\frac{1}{3} = 2\frac{?}{42}$. Divide 3 into 42 to get 14 and then multiply by the 1 in the numerator to get $2\frac{1}{3} = 2\frac{14}{42}$. Similarly, $\frac{9}{14} = \frac{?}{42}$. Divide 14 into 42 to get 3 and then multiply this by 9 in the numerator to get $\frac{9}{14} = \frac{27}{42}$. Now, since the denominators are the same, $2\frac{14}{42} + \frac{27}{42}$, add the two numerators to get $2\frac{41}{42}$. The answer is (d).

39. Since the first delay is $\frac{3}{4}$ of an hour, and the second delay is $1\frac{1}{2}$ hours, add these two numbers together to get the total delay. Since the common denominator is 4, rewrite $1\frac{1}{2}$ with a denominator of 4, $1\frac{1}{2} = 1\frac{?}{4}$. Divide 2 into 4 and multiply this number by 1 in the numerator to get $1\frac{1}{2} = 1\frac{2}{4}$. Leave $\frac{3}{4}$ as is. Now add $\frac{3}{4} + 1\frac{2}{4}$ to get $1\frac{5}{4}$. Change $\frac{5}{4}$ to a mixed number of $1\frac{1}{4}$ and add $1 + 1\frac{1}{4}$ to equal $2\frac{1}{4}$ hours. If you add 2 hours to 10:00 A.M., you will get 12:00 noon. Then add 15 more minutes, which is the equivalent to $\frac{1}{4}$ of an hour, ($\frac{1}{4} \times 60 = 15$) to get a blast off time of 12:15 P.M. The answer is (c).

40. A) Find $\frac{2}{5}$ of 1000 minutes to see how many minutes were used so far. Multiply $\frac{2}{5} \times 1000$. Use canceling to divide 5 into both 5 and 1000, $\frac{2}{1\cancel{5}} \times \cancel{1000}^{200}$. Multiply what is left to get 400 minutes. Your answer is (a).

    B) Subtract $1000 - 400$ to get 600 minutes left for the rest of the month. Your answer is (b).

41. To find the better buy, you must find the unit price for the oranges at each store and choose the lower price. To find Ricky's price at A & S Convenience Store, divide $2.96 by 3 to get $.9866 . . . per pound. To find Marty's price at Peppy's Market, divide $4.85 by 5 to get $.97 per pound. Since Marty's unit price is less than Ricky's, Marty's is the better buy. The answer is (b).

42. A) First, subtract $170 from $500 to find how much money remained after spending, $500 - $170 = $330. Next, find $\frac{2}{3}$ of $330 using multiplication, $\frac{2}{3} \times 330$. Use canceling to divide 3 into both 3 and 330, $\frac{2}{1\cancel{3}} \times \cancel{330}^{110}$. Multiply what's left to get $220. Then divide $220 by 4 to find out how much each charity will get. $220 ÷ 4 = $55 for each charity. The answer is (c).

    B) Add $170 + $220 to get $390, which represents the total money spent and given to charity. Subtract $390 from $500, $500 - $390 to get $110, which is the money left for savings. The answer is (b).

43. Rewrite $1\frac{1}{2}$ as the improper fraction $\frac{3}{2}$.

Then, multiply $\overset{11}{\cancel{22}} \times \frac{3}{\underset{1}{\cancel{2}}}$. Use canceling to divide 2 into both 2 and 22 in the diagonal direction, $22 \div 2 = 11$ and $2 \div 2 = 1$. The problem now looks like $11 \times \frac{3}{1}$. Multiply 11×3 to get $33. The answer is (b).

44. To find the price of meal special B, multiply $\frac{2}{3} \times 4.44$. Use canceling to divide 3 into both 3 and 4.44, $\frac{2}{\underset{1}{\cancel{3}}} \times \overset{1.48}{\cancel{4.44}}$. Multiply what's left to get $2.96. The answer is (b).

45. A) Multiply $\frac{1}{2} \times 276$ to see how many children choose baseball. Use canceling to divide 2 into both 2 and 276, $\frac{1}{\underset{1}{\cancel{2}}} \times \overset{138}{\cancel{276}}$. Multiply what's left to get 138. The answer is (d).

B) There are two ways to do this problem:

For the first way, multiply $\frac{3}{4} \times 276$ to see how many children did choose swimming for week 2. Use canceling to divide 4 into both 4 and 276, $\frac{3}{\underset{1}{\cancel{4}}} \times \overset{69}{\cancel{276}}$. Multiply what's left to get 207. Then subtract 207 from 276 to find out how many children did not choose swimming for week 2, $276 - 207 = 69$. The answer is (b).

For the second way, subtract $\frac{3}{4}$ from 1 whole to see what fractional part of the children did not choose swimming for week 2. Rewrite 1 as $\frac{4}{4}$ (since the denominator of $\frac{3}{4}$ is 4). Now subtract, $\frac{4}{4} - \frac{3}{4} = \frac{1}{4}$. $\frac{1}{4}$ of the children did not choose swimming. Next multiply $\frac{1}{4} \times 276$. Use canceling to divide 4 into both 4 and 276, $\frac{1}{\underset{1}{\cancel{4}}} \times \overset{69}{\cancel{276}}$. The answer is 69 (b).

ANSWERS TO PICNIC LIST, PAGE 199

1. To adjust the picnic list for 20 family members (two times the original), double each item on the picnic list by multiplying each item by 2.

   $\frac{1}{2}$ lb salami

   $1\frac{1}{3}$ lb bologna

   $1\frac{1}{2}$ lb turkey

   3 lb corned beef

   1 lb pastrami

   $2\frac{2}{3}$ lb roast beef

   $2\frac{1}{2}$ lb potato salad

   $5\frac{1}{3}$ lb cole slaw

   4 dozen rolls (48)

   5 lb fruit salad

   6 lb cookies

2. To adjust the picnic list for 30 family members (three times the original), triple each item on the picnic list by multiplying each item by 3.

   $\frac{3}{4}$ lb salami

   2 lb bologna

   $2\frac{1}{4}$ lb turkey

   $4\frac{1}{2}$ lb corned beef

   $1\frac{1}{2}$ lb pastrami

4 lb roast beef

$3\frac{3}{4}$ lb potato salad

8 lb cole slaw

6 dozen rolls (72)

$7\frac{1}{2}$ lb fruit salad

9 lb cookies

3. To adjust the picnic list for 5 family members (one half the original), multiply each item on the picnic list by $\frac{1}{2}$.

$\frac{1}{8}$ lb salami

$\frac{1}{3}$ lb bologna

$\frac{3}{8}$ lb turkey

$\frac{3}{4}$ lb corned beef

$\frac{1}{4}$ lb pastrami

$\frac{2}{3}$ lb roast beef

$\frac{5}{8}$ lb potato salad

$1\frac{1}{3}$ lb cole slaw

1 dozen rolls (12)

$1\frac{1}{4}$ lb fruit salad

$1\frac{1}{2}$ lb cookies

ANSWERS TO PUZZLING FRACTIONS

Puzzling Fractions #1, page 200

They both go to the top!

Puzzling Fractions #2, pages 201–202

They both make a part!

Puzzling Fractions #3, pages 203–205

They both follow an order!

ANSWERS TO INCORRECT
SOLUTIONS, PAGES 206–209

1. You can't add fraction numerators and denominators. You must first find an LCD of 40 since 5 and 8 divide into 40 evenly. Then, change $1\frac{3}{5}$ into $1\frac{24}{40}$ by dividing 5 into 40 and multiplying 8 by the old numerator of 3. Then change $2\frac{3}{8}$ into $2\frac{15}{40}$ by dividing 8 into 40 and multiplying 5 by the old numerator of 3. Then, add your whole numbers and your numerators, but keep your denominator as 40.

$$1\frac{24}{40} + 2\frac{15}{40} = 3\frac{39}{40}$$

The answer is $3\frac{39}{40}$.

2. 4 is the GCF (Greatest Common Factor) of 8 and 12. The LCM is the lowest number that 8 and 12 divide into evenly, so that number is 24.

3. 5 does divide evenly into both 5 and 10, but $\frac{4}{1\overline{5}} \times \frac{\overset{2}{\cancel{10}}}{11} = \frac{8}{11}$.

The 5 in the denominator doesn't stay a 5. It becomes a 1.

4. Multiply $\frac{5}{8}$ by 576, not $\frac{3}{8} \times 576$. $\frac{5}{8} \times 576$ can be changed to $\frac{5}{1\overline{8}} \times \cancel{576}^{72}$ since 8 divides evenly into both 8 and 576. Then, multiply 5 times 72 to get 360. Joella read 360 pages. 216 is the number of pages still left to read.

5. When fractions are changed into their equivalent forms, $\frac{1}{3}$ should equal $\frac{4}{12}$ instead of $\frac{5}{12}$, since 3 goes into 12 four times and then, 1 times 4 = 4. So, now add $\frac{9}{12} + \frac{4}{12} + 1\frac{6}{12} = 1\frac{19}{12}$. Divide 12 into 19 to get $1\frac{7}{12}$ and add this to the 1 that is already there. Your answer is $2\frac{7}{12}$.

6. To change $4\frac{1}{2}$ to an improper fraction after you multiply 2 by 4, you have to add 1 to this number to get a numerator of 9. The improper fraction will be $\frac{9}{2}$. Now, to divide 36 by $\frac{9}{2}$, flip $\frac{9}{2}$ over to its reciprocal and multiply 36 by $\frac{2}{9}$. 9 divides evenly into both 9 and 36, $\overset{4}{36} \times \frac{2}{\underset{1}{9}}$. Multiply to get an answer of 8 months.

7. a) The three denominators do not divide evenly into 16. Instead, 24 is the LCD because all denominators can divide evenly into 24. Change each fraction into its equivalent form, and total the number of inches of rain.

$4\frac{1}{2} = 4\frac{12}{24}, 3\frac{1}{6} = 3\frac{4}{24}, 1\frac{7}{8} = 1\frac{21}{24}$

$4\frac{12}{24} + 3\frac{4}{24} + 1\frac{21}{24} = 8\frac{37}{24}$

Divide 24 into 37 to get $1\frac{13}{24}$ which will be added to the 8 to get $8 + 1\frac{13}{24} = 9\frac{13}{24}$ inches of rain.

b) Since $8\frac{15}{16}$ is the incorrect solution to part a), it should not be part of the b) solution. Instead, subtract $9\frac{13}{24}$ from 15,

$15 - 9\frac{13}{24}$.

Change 15 into $14\frac{24}{24}$, and then subtract $9\frac{13}{24}$ from it. Subtract the whole numbers and the fraction numerators to get $14\frac{24}{24} - 9\frac{13}{24} = 5\frac{11}{24}$ inches of rain.

8. After the fractions are lined up with the same denominator, you must rewrite the top fraction so that it will be larger than $\frac{2}{4}$ by borrowing $1 = \frac{4}{4}$ from the 11 and adding it to the $\frac{1}{4}$.

$11\frac{1}{4} = 10\frac{5}{4}, 10\frac{5}{4} - 8\frac{2}{4}$

Now subtract the whole numbers and the fraction numerators,

$10\frac{5}{4} - 8\frac{2}{4} = 2\frac{3}{4}$.

The correct answer is $2\frac{3}{4}$.

9. Set up your proportion as

$$\frac{total\ price}{number\ of\ hours} = \frac{total\ price}{number\ of\ hours}$$

Replace the price and number of hours as follows:

$\frac{\$127.50}{15} = \frac{p}{20}$ ($127.50 and 15 hours go together, and 20 hours and the unknown price go together: we'll call the total price p.) Multiply the cross products to get $15 \times p = \$127.50 \times 20$ or $15p = \$2550$. Divide 15 into 2550 to get an answer of $170.

10. Expand $\left(\frac{1}{3}\right)^3 \left(\frac{2}{9}\right) (3)^2$ to equal $\frac{1}{3} \times \frac{1}{3} \times \frac{1}{3} \times \frac{2}{9} \times 3 \times 3$.

Cancel two of the 3s in the denominator with the two 3s in the numerator, $\frac{1}{1\cancel{3}} \times \frac{1}{1\cancel{3}} \times \frac{1}{3} \times \frac{2}{9} \times \cancel{3}^1 \times \cancel{3}^1$. You can't cancel all three 3s in the denominator with the two 3s in the numerator. You should still have a 3 left in the denominator. Multiply the remaining numerators and denominators $\frac{1 \times 1 \times 1 \times 2}{3 \times 9}$, to equal $\frac{2}{27}$.

ANSWER TO WORD SEARCH, PAGE 210

Find these words in the following table of letters below:

Denominator
Numerator
Multiply
Divide
Add
Subtract
Cancel
Simplify
Fraction
Reciprocal
Ratio
Factor

D	S	S	R	O	T	C	A	F	D	R
I	R	I	U	O	P	A	T	A	N	O
L	N	M	M	B	I	T	R	N	U	T
A	C	P	O	M	T	O	A	O	M	A
C	D	L	T	I	A	R	C	I	E	N
O	E	I	R	N	N	R	A	T	R	I
R	O	F	V	A	N	D	D	C	A	M
P	I	Y	A	I	S	A	A	A	T	O
I	T	S	I	T	D	N	M	R	O	N
C	A	D	E	D	C	E	P	F	R	E
E	R	D	M	E	V	L	U	C	T	D
R	E	Y	L	P	I	T	L	U	M	N

CHAPTER TWELVE

Family Activities with Fractions

Activities for your family to do
That will put a smile on all of you.

FAMILY ACTIVITIES WITH FRACTIONS

There are many fun family hands-on activities that can be done at home or outside of the home in everyday life that will help your children see fractions are "painless."

Here are just a few:

Sorting Objects

Tell children to separate items such as toys, books, pencils, food, or packages into piles. 2 piles represent $\frac{1}{2}$ of the items in each pile, 4 piles represent $\frac{1}{4}$ of the items in each pile, and so on. Piles can be organized by colors, type of item, equal parts among siblings, and so forth, and different fractional parts will result.

Pizza

Order a pizza. Cut it into 8 slices. Show that:

1 slice $= \frac{1}{8}$ of the pizza

3 slices $= \frac{3}{8}$ of the pizza

8 slices $= \frac{8}{8} = 1$ whole pizza

(Refer to Chapter 1, pages 3 and 17.)

Marbles or Candy

Use 50 marbles or pieces of candy.

A) Tell your children to separate them into equal groups. What combinations of groups could you have?

(You could have 5 groups of 10, 10 groups of 5, 2 groups of 25, 25 groups of 2, 1 group of 50, or 50 groups of 1.) (Refer to Chapter 1, page 11.)

B) Go back to the 50 candies/marbles. Tell your children to take $\frac{1}{5}$ away. How many will they take away? How many are left?

(Multiply $\frac{1}{5} \times 50$. You will have 10 to take away and $50 - 10 = 40$ left.

If you take $\frac{2}{5}$ away, you will multiply $\frac{2}{5} \times 50$ to get 20 and $50 - 20 = 30$ left.) (Refer to Chapter 3, pages 53–54.)

Use various number combinations of marbles or candy to keep changing the activity each time.

Money

Use fractions to explain parts of a dollar. Since a dollar equals 100 cents, take 100 pennies and show:

50 pennies out of 100 pennies or $\frac{50}{100} = \frac{1}{2}$ of a dollar
(i.e., a half dollar = 50 cents)

25 pennies out of 100 pennies or $\frac{25}{100} = \frac{1}{4}$ of a dollar
(i.e., a quarter dollar = 25 cents)

10 pennies out of 100 pennies or $\frac{10}{100} = \frac{1}{10}$ of a dollar

(i.e., a dime = 10 cents) (Refer to Chapter 1, page 17.)

Continue in a similar manner to show other fractional penny arrangements.

Time and the Clock

A) Hours, Minutes, Seconds

Introduce 60 seconds in a minute and 60 minutes in an hour. Discuss:

1) What part of a minute is a second? $\left(\frac{1}{60}\right)$

2) What part of an hour is 30 minutes? $\left(\frac{30}{60} = \frac{1}{2} \text{ hour}\right)$

3) $\frac{3}{4}$ of an hour is how many minutes? $\left(\frac{3}{4} \times 60\right) = 45$ minutes

(Refer to Chapter 1, page 17 and Chapter 3, pages 53–54.)

Continue in a similar manner with other seconds and minutes.

B) Using a Clock Face (You can use a real one or have the children make one out of construction paper with movable hands.)

Demonstrate that a clock face has 12 big numbers on it. (Each number represents 1 hour with the small "hour" hand and 5 minutes of a 60-minute hour with the big "minute" hand. Some clocks also have a "second" hand.)

To illustrate fractions on the clock, let's work with the big hand:

If the big hand moves from 12 to 1, what part of an hour has passed? $\left(\frac{5 \text{ minutes}}{60 \text{ minutes}} = \frac{1}{12} \text{ of an hour.} \right)$

If the big hand moves from 12 to 2, what part of an hour has passed? (Each time the clock moves to another large number, $\frac{5 \text{ minutes}}{60 \text{ minutes}} = \frac{1}{12}$ of an hour has passed, so here $\frac{10 \text{ minutes}}{60 \text{ minutes}} = \frac{1}{6}$ of an hour has passed from 12 to 2.)

If the big hand moves from 12 to 6, what part of an hour has passed? $\left(\frac{30 \text{ minutes}}{60 \text{ minutes}} = \frac{6}{12} = \frac{1}{2} \text{ of an hour has passed from 12 to 6.} \right)$

Have the children move the hands and make up their own problems.

After the children can work with the hands of the clock face, introduce addition of fractions here. For example, what is $\frac{1}{4}$ of an hour added to $\frac{1}{5}$ of an hour?

$\left(\frac{1}{4} + \frac{1}{5} = \frac{5}{20} + \frac{4}{20} = \frac{9}{20} \text{ of an hour or } \frac{9}{20} \times 60 = 27 \text{ minutes.} \right)$

Also, how about subtraction? If $\frac{1}{10}$ or $\frac{10}{60} = 6$ minutes of an hour have passed, how much time is left to reach a whole hour?

$$\left(1 - \frac{1}{10} = \frac{10}{10} - \frac{1}{10} = \frac{9}{10} \text{ of an hour or } \frac{9}{10} \times 60 = 54 \text{ minutes.}\right)$$

Also, 60 minutes − 6 minutes = 54 minutes. (Refer to Chapter 1, page 17, Chapter 3, pages 53–54, Chapter 5, pages 77–84, and Chapter 6, pages 93–102.)

Folding Paper

Take a rectangular piece of paper and fold it in half. Fold it in half again. Fold it in half a third time. Open it up each time to see the number of sections and the size of each fractional part.

NUMBER OF FOLDS	NUMBER OF SECTIONS	WHAT PART OF THE WHOLE PAPER IS EACH SECTION?
1	2	$\frac{1}{2}$
2	4	$\frac{1}{4}$
3	8	$\frac{1}{8}$
4	16	$\frac{1}{16}$
5	32	$\frac{1}{32}$

Continue in the same way with different numbers of folds.

Measuring Spoons and Cups

Measuring spoons and cups can be used to illustrate fractional size and equivalencies. They can be used in the bathtub with plain water, in the summer on the beach with sand, outside in the winter with snow, or in the kitchen to measure ingredients.

Use measuring spoons and cups in different sizes, some of which are $\frac{1}{8}$ teaspoon, $\frac{1}{4}$ teaspoon, $\frac{1}{2}$ teaspoon, 1 tablespoon, $\frac{1}{4}$ cup, $\frac{1}{2}$ cup, and so on. Equivalent measurements can be shown

here if all spoons/cups are in the same units, that is, 2 of the $\frac{1}{8}$ teaspoons are equivalent to 1 of the $\frac{1}{4}$ teaspoons and 2 of the $\frac{1}{4}$ cups are equal to 1 of the $\frac{1}{2}$ cups. Since there are 8 ounces in a cup, what part of a cup is 6 ounces? (It is $\frac{6}{8} = \frac{3}{4}$ cups.) Also, since 3 teaspoons are equal to 1 tablespoon, what part of a tablespoon is 1 teaspoon? (It is equal to $\frac{1}{3}$ of a tablespoon.)

Continue with other spoon and cup measurements in a similar fashion.

Recipe

Bake chocolate chip cookies. Use a favorite recipe with some or all fractional ingredients. For example, if a recipe for chocolate chip cookies lists 1 cup of shortening to make 48 cookies, how many cups of shortening will make 24 cookies? (To make 24 cookies, use $\dfrac{1 \text{ cup of shortening}}{48 \text{ cookies}} = \dfrac{\frac{1}{2} \text{ cup of shortening}}{24 \text{ cookies}}$. (Refer to Chapter 9, pages 152–153.)

How much shortening for 96 cookies? (To make 96 cookies, use $\dfrac{1 \text{ cup of shortening}}{48 \text{ cookies}} = \dfrac{2 \text{ cups of shortening}}{96 \text{ cookies}}$.)

Suppose the recipe also lists $2\frac{1}{2}$ cups sifted all-purpose flour for 48 cookies, how much flour would you need for only 12 cookies?

(Use a proportion to set up $\dfrac{2\frac{1}{2}\text{ cups flour}}{48\text{ cookies}} = \dfrac{x\text{(cups flour)}}{12\text{ cookies}}$ and cross multiply to solve for x.) (Refer to Chapter 9, pages 150–153.)

$$12\left(2\frac{1}{2}\right) = (48)(x)$$

$$12 \times \frac{5}{2} = 48x$$

$$30 = 48x$$

$$30 \div 48 = \frac{30}{48}$$

Divide both numerator and denominator by 6 to get $x = \dfrac{5}{8}$ cup of flour.

Use other recipe ingredients to set up similar proportions and find corresponding ingredients for different sized recipes. Enjoy baking the cookies or a similar favorite delicious recipe!

Picnic

Plan a family picnic. Refer to page 199 as a guide and plan a picnic for your family.

Shopping

Take your family shopping.

A) Toy Store

Take your children to a toy store. If your child has $10.00 to spend in the toy store and chooses a doll for $8.50, what fractional part of the $10 will your child spend? $\left(\dfrac{8.50}{10.00}\right.$ can be reduced by 10 since 10 divides evenly into both the numerator and denominator, $\dfrac{8.50}{10.00} = \dfrac{.85}{1.00}$. Then, divide 5 into both .85 and 1.00 to get $\dfrac{.17}{.20}$. Finally, drop the decimal points since they are both in cents, to get an answer of $\left.\dfrac{17}{20}.\right)$ (Refer to Chapter 9, page 142, #9 and page 156, #9.)

How much money does your child have left to spend, and what fractional part does this represent? (Subtract $10 − $8.50 to get $1.50 left. Subtract $1 - \frac{17}{20} = \frac{20}{20} - \frac{17}{20} = \frac{3}{20}$ of the money left as a fractional part.) (Refer to Chapter 6, pages 96–97.)

B) Grocery Store

Have your children help you make purchases at the grocery store. First, have them help you make up the shopping list. If one of the items on your list is $1\frac{1}{4}$ pounds of deli turkey and another item is $\frac{3}{4}$ pound of cheese, how much would they both cost if turkey costs $1.50 for $\frac{1}{4}$ of a pound and cheese costs $.80 for $\frac{1}{4}$ of a pound? ($1\frac{1}{4}$ pounds $= \frac{5}{4}$ pounds $= 5 \times \frac{1}{4}$ pound, so $1.50 × 5 = $7.50 for the turkey. $\frac{3}{4}$ pound $=$ 3 times $\frac{1}{4}$ pound, so $.80 × 3 = $2.40 for the cheese. The total bill for these two items is $7.50 + $2.40 = $9.90.)

Vary your purchases and the item amounts and have children locate the store items, compare prices, and use fractions in some of the transactions.

The Ruler

Show your children the ruler. Most rulers have each inch split into 16 parts with markings for each half, fourth, eighth, and sixteenth. Show how big each part is on the ruler. Explain and show how 2 of the $\frac{1}{8}$ sections are equal to 1 of the $\frac{1}{4}$ sections, and 4 of the $\frac{1}{8}$ sections are equal to 1 of the $\frac{1}{2}$ sections.

Next, show that if you start at $\frac{1}{4}$ of an inch and move over $\frac{1}{8}$ of an inch to the right, you will end up at $\frac{3}{8}$ of an inch (because

$\frac{1}{4} + \frac{1}{8} = \frac{2}{8} + \frac{1}{8} = \frac{3}{8}$). Also, if you start at $1\frac{1}{2}$ inches and move to

the right $\frac{3}{4}$ of an inch, you will arrive at $2\frac{1}{4}$ inches (because $1\frac{1}{2} +$

$\frac{3}{4} = 1\frac{2}{4} + \frac{3}{4} = 1\frac{5}{4} = 2\frac{1}{4}$ inches). (Refer to Chapter 5, pages 77–84.)

Likewise, if you start at $3\frac{3}{4}$ inches and go to the left $\frac{3}{8}$ of an

inch, you will end up at $3\frac{3}{8}$ inches (because $3\frac{3}{4} - \frac{3}{8} = 3\frac{6}{8} - \frac{3}{8} =$

$3\frac{3}{8}$ inches). (Refer to Chapter 6, pages 93–102.)

Continue using the ruler to show various other equivalent combinations of fractional measurements and addition and subtraction problems.

In the House

Count the rooms in your house with your children. Then, have them go through the house and see how many rooms have beds, tables, windows, televisions, and so on.

If your house has 8 rooms and 3 rooms have beds, what

fractional part of the rooms have beds? $\left(\frac{3}{8}\right)$ If 4 rooms have

tables, what fractional part of the rooms have tables?

$$\left(\frac{4}{8} = \frac{1}{2}\right)$$

Continue choosing objects for the children to find throughout the house and change the objects each time you do this family activity.

Amusement Park

Take your family to an amusement park. Have your children help purchase tickets, figure out prices, choose the better buy, and find fractional parts.

Suppose 1 ride ticket costs $1.50, 10 tickets cost $10, 20 tickets cost $18, and a book of 100 tickets costs $80.

A) How much do you save per ride ticket by buying the book of 100 tickets over a single-ride ticket price? ($80 ÷ 100 = $.80 per ticket, so $1.50 − $.80 = $.70 savings over the single-price ticket.) What fractional part of the single-price ticket does the $.80 represent? $\left(\frac{.80}{1.50} = \frac{.08}{.15}\right.$ by dividing both numerator and denominator by 10. Then drop the cents and your fraction will simplify to $\left.\frac{8}{15}.\right)$ (Refer to Chapter 9, page 142, #9 and page 156, #9.)

B) If cotton candy costs 2 single tickets or $2.75, have your children figure out which is a better buy. (Since each single ticket is $1.50, the price using 2 tickets would be $1.50 × 2 = $3.00. If you use cash, the price is $2.75, so cash is a better buy for $2.75.)

C) Finally, if you buy the book of 100 tickets, and it costs 6 tickets for the roller coaster ride for each child, what fractional part of the 100 tickets would it cost for 2 children to go on the roller coaster? (6 + 6 = 12 tickets and $\frac{12}{100} = \frac{3}{25}$ by dividing both numerator and denominator by 4.) (Refer to Chapter 1, page 17.)

Continue making up similar problems for your children to work on while enjoying themselves at the amusement park.

Fractions Resources on the Web

Kids Online resources
http://www.kidsolr.com/math/fractions.html
Explanations, puzzles

AAA Math
http://www.aaamath.com
Explanations, interactive practice, challenging games

Funbrain Fresh Baked Fractions
http://www.funbrain.com/fract
Fun games

Math Forum
http://mathforum.org/paths/fractions/
A tour of fractions
Dr. Math's questions and answers about fractions

Math.com
The world of math online
*http://www.math.com/homeworkhelp/HotSubjects_*
    fractions.html
Practice problems, including quizzes

EDHelper.com
http://www.edhelper.com/fractions.htm
Fractions!!
Addition, subtraction, multiplication, division
Fraction puzzles
Algebraic fractions
Worksheets, puzzles (including Sudoku)

Purple Math
Fractions review
http://www.purplemath.com/modules/
Explanations

Fractions
http://www.mathleague.com/help/help.htm
Tutorials

Coolmath (ages 3–12)
http://www.coolmath4kids.com/fractions/index.html
Math amusement and learning

Coolmath (ages 13–100)
http://www.coolmath.com
Math amusement and learning

Sheppard Software
*www.sheppardsoftware.com/mathgames/fractions/
    fracTut1.htm*
Math games: fractions tutorial

HomeSchoolMath
www.homeschoolmath.net/online/fractions.php
Fraction games and tutorials online

Kids Math Blog
www.kidsmathblog.com/fractions-kids
Easy to follow guide, worksheets and tips for parents and
    teachers about math for kids

Visual Fractions
www.visualfractions.com
A tutorial that models fractions with number lines or circles

Math Warehouse
*http://www.mathwarehouse.com/fractions/fraction-
    tutorial/fraction-tutorial.php*
A visual tutorial on what a fraction is

Tutors 4 You
http://tutors4you.com/tutorialonfractions.htm
Tutorial on fractions

Johnnie's Math Page
http://jmathpage.com/JIMSFractionsrecognizecompare.html
Fun math for kids and their teachers

Equivalent Fractions Games
http://www.free-training-tutorial.com/equivalent-
fractions-games.html
Interactive activities for teaching equivalent fractions, online
practice for elementary students

MathIsFun
http://www.mathsisfun.com/fractions_addition.html
Adding fractions

INDEX

Get access to your exclusive PAINLESS FRACTIONS mobile app

Just visit *www.BarronsBooks.com/painless.html*

To face the ultimate Fractions and Arcade Action Game Challenge!

A
for eve

www.ba
There
how t
contai
knowle
arca

ON'S

ESS

ns